DISCIPLINE, GRIEVANCE AND DISMISSAL

DISCIPLINE, GRIEVANCE AND DISMISSAL

A Manager's Pocket Guide

Sue Morris

The Industrial Society

First published in 1993 by
The Industrial Society
Robert Hyde House
48 Bryanston Square
London W1H 7LN
Telephone: 071-262 2401

© *The Industrial Society 1993*
Reprinted 1995

ISBN 0 85290 884 9

British Library Cataloguing-in-Publication Data.
A catalogue record for this book is available from the
British Library.

Typeset by: The Midlands Book Typesetting Company
Printed by: Formara Limited

Cover design: Rhodes Design
Text illustrations: Sophie Grillet

Contents

Introduction

The aim of this booklet is to provide basic guidelines for employers when dealing with matters of Discipline, Dismissal and Grievance.

The procedures and policies suggested can be readily adapted to suit any size or type of organisation and are intended to provide practical, down to earth advice for all levels of management from the first line supervisor to the Chief Executive.

Although there is a legal requirement to provide formal Discipline and Grievance Procedures where sufficient numbers of people are employed, it is recommended that they are provided for any size of operation, no matter how small.

Discipline should not be regarded as a means whereby employees are coerced, punished or eventually dismissed but rather as a way of helping the employee to be able to meet the requirements of the organisation by providing advice, guidance and training.

Use of the Grievance Procedure by an employee should not be perceived as a threat but more as a plea for help from an individual who has failed to get his/her complaint or concern listened to by informal means.

The objective of providing Discipline and Grievance Procedures is to enhance productive working relationships by providing established and logical means for dealing with problems as they arise, whether from the employer or employee's point of view, so that they are dealt with quickly and amicably before mountains are made out of molehills!

Effective procedures will only be achieved by ensuring that the principles contained in them are acceptable and logical and that all employees including those responsible for administering them are properly informed and trained in their use.

1 Discipline

What is meant by Discipline?

The Shorter Oxford English Dictionary includes in its definition of "discipline"

1 Instruction imparted to disciples or scholars; teaching; learning
2 A branch of instruction; a department of knowledge
3 The training of subordinates to proper conduct and action by instructing them in the same; mental and moral training
4 A system of rules for conduct
5 Correction; chastisement

Sadly the most common definition understood by many employers and employees is "chastisement"!

Discipline, therefore, is about setting standards of behaviour and performance, letting people know what those standards are, helping people to achieve and maintain those standards by example, by training, by guidance and letting them know what action they can expect to be taken if they fail to meet those standards.

Examples of standards:

- Acceptable levels of attendance, e.g. timekeeping, days of sickness
- Acceptable levels of performance, e.g. accuracy, speed of work
- Acceptable performance in winning new orders or customers
- Acceptable behaviour in the workplace when dealing with colleagues or customers

Establishing good standards of behaviour and performance

At Recruitment

Making people aware of an organisation's expectations and standards starts even before an employee has joined an organisation. It is important to make prospective employees aware of the standards that are expected in terms of job performance as well as general conduct.

For example,

At interview, when describing the duties the prospective employee will be required to perform, the interviewer should make it clear what is expected, e.g.

- an order picker might be expected to be able to pick at least an average of 200 orders a day with an accuracy ratio of at least 195/200 to meet acceptable standards of performance

- a customer services clerk in a busy sales office must be able to handle tactfully any number of irate and irrational customers without joining in the battle!
- where employees work as part of a dedicated team or have specific handover duties at the start and end of shifts poor time-keeping may well be more of a serious problem than in a situation where there is flexible working.

Whatever the organisation's requirements are they should be spelt out to the prospective employee at interview so that they understand before making their decision to accept employment what conditions they will be working under and what standards they will be expected to maintain.

At Induction

Starting a new job for any employee, whether a school or college leaver or someone who has been in employment for many years is a traumatic experience. There are new codes of conduct, new expectations as well as new duties to contend with. Whatever the level, from the most junior employee to the most senior it is important that the new-comer is introduced to the requirements of the organisation in a planned and effective manner. If the employee is not made aware of the requirements then the employer is in no position to complain if the employee does not meet them!

The Induction Programme is the ideal opportunity to ensure that the ground rules are set from "day one" so that the new employee is fully acquainted with all the company's rules and regulations, the general terms and conditions of employment, codes of conduct, company philosophy as well as all other matters affecting their employment.

A good induction programme will not try to cram all this

information into the first day of employment but will arrange a programme so that the newcomer is briefed over a planned period of days in the early weeks of employment. This will enable the essential issues to be addressed first, on say the first day of work, whilst arranging for the remaining issues to be addressed in an organised manner but more gradually so that the new employee has the opportunity of absorbing the information rather than being overwhelmed on the first day with a whole host of information which they could not possibly be expected to remember.

The object of the Induction Programme is to:

■ Help an employee quickly to feel at home and part of the team:
■ Introduce a new employee to work colleagues and show them where the key locations are for their early days in employment (work stations, loos, canteen, etc).
■ Make people aware of what the organisation's business is all about and how their particular job fits in.
■ Understand the structure of the organisation and the reporting and functional lines of responsibility.

Explain Rules and Regulations, e.g.:

■ what happens if they report late for work
■ what they must do if they are off sick
■ how to arrange their holidays
■ arrangements for overtime working

Explain Health and Safety Regulations, e.g.:

■ what to do if they have an accident
■ fire procedures
■ particular safety requirements relating to their equipment
■ wearing of protective clothing

Explain Security Arrangements, e.g.:

- wearing of identity badges
- the company's right to search employees or their property
- checking in and out of visitors
- any security restricted access areas

Explain Disciplinary and Grievance Procedures, e.g.:

- a description of the procedures
- the type of offences that will constitute misconduct
- the type of offences that will consititute gross misconduct
- who they should contact in the event of a grievance

To learn about one's new duties, e.g.:

- To be trained in the requirements of the job either by informal discussion, informal training or coaching or by a formal training scheme.
- To avoid misunderstandings a job description should be provided.

Job Descriptions

The purpose of providing an employee with a job description is twofold:

1 to provide a basic description of the job itself and its key elements

   This will include:

   - who the employee reports to
   - who the employee is responsible for
   - regular contacts both inside and outside the organisation
   - a brief summary of each of the key activities of the job
   - the limits of authority which apply, e.g. expenditure, products, people

2 to describe the ongoing standards that must be achieved in those activities to be able to say that an acceptable work performance is being maintained

   This will include the measures that will be applied to the activities in terms of:

   - time taken to achieve the activity
   - percentages of loss or gain, etc.

Ideally, when putting together a new job description, it is the employee who is best informed to prepare the first draft which should then be discussed and agreed by the line manager.

If a new employee is being taken on into an established job then clearly it is important for the employee to understand and accept what is required by the job description before agreeing to take up the post.

By ensuring that the employee knows what is required of him/her, both in terms of the duties and the standard to which those duties must be performed, then any difficulties which the employee is experiencing in meeting the requirements can be raised and hopefully put right at an early stage before the matter escalates to the need to consider disciplinary action because of poor performance.

Informal One-to-One Meetings

Whether or not there is a formal appraisal scheme in place it is important for both employee and supervisor or line manager to meet on a regular one-to-one basis to review and monitor performance and to discuss and resolve any issues that might be creating problems before they become major difficulties.

Most line management will claim that they talk to their employees informally on a regular basis but such discussions are likely to be somewhat one-sided and superficial. However by setting aside a regular block of time and both parties consciously putting together an agenda of items they wish to discuss, such meetings will prove to be very effective and rewarding.

Appraisals

It is important that all employees' performance is appraised on a regular basis so that:

- employees know how they are getting on and whether they are meeting expectations
- the job description can be reviewed and updated if necessary
- they can be offered guidance and if necessary further training or coaching if there are areas of performance

which need improving or even extending to cover a wider range of activities

- the employee's expectations and aspirations can be identified to see whether there are future career opportunities which can be worked towards
- the employee is given the opportunity, without fear of reprisal, of offering his/her views on matters concerning his/her work, e.g. better ways of handling certain activities or even difficulties which he/she might be experiencing that are unknown to the appraiser.
- a formal follow-up interview may be agreed to ensure that any targets or objectives set are carried out and not forgotten.

Appraisal schemes frequently allow for a formal appraisal interview on a "once a year basis" where the employee and line manager will set aside a period of time in which to review the above mentioned matters. Following each formal appraisal interview there should be on-going reviews so that the matters discussed can be followed up to ensure that progress is being made and that any actions that were agreed actually happen.

For example, if an employee is having difficulty with coming to grips with a particular aspect of his/her work then it may have been agreed at the appraisal interview that a formal training course would be provided or perhaps time would be set aside with another colleague so that coaching could be undertaken. If a review date is not set it is all too easy for these plans to be forgotten by the appraiser who will be in no position to complain if the employee's performance continues to fail to come up to scratch! In the above example it would also be important for both the appraisee and appraiser to be able to assess and discuss whether the help provided was effective or whether alternative arrangements need to be considered. By failing to follow up action points agreed at the appraisal interview the employer leaves him/herself wide open to unfair treatment of the employee if the matter progresses to disciplinary action and ultimately dismissal for poor performance.

Even though there may be a formal appraisal scheme in place it is still the responsibility of line management to ensure that employees are informally appraised on an ongoing regular basis so that any problems or difficulties are addressed immediately and can be rectified quickly before the matter escalates into a bigger problem.

By addressing problems and difficulties as they occur there is every likelihood that the matter can be corrected without the need to resort to formal disciplinary action.

Requirement to provide Disciplinary Rules and Procedures

All employers are required by law to supply written details of the disciplinary rules and procedures if:

- they employ 20 or more employees, working 16 hours or more per week on the date that their continuous service began, then such details must be supplied within 13 weeks of starting employment
  or if
- they employ 20 or more employees, working at least 8 but less than 16 hours per week on the date that their continuous service began, then such details must be supplied within 13 weeks of completing five years' service.

For employers who employ less than 20 employees, even though there is no statutory requirement to supply particulars of the disciplinary rules and procedures to their employees, it is recommended that they do, so that all employees know where they stand.

A Code of Practice has been issued by the Advisory, Conciliation and Arbitration Service (ACAS) entitled Disciplinary Practice and Procedures in Employment. Although the Code of Practice is not legally binding, Industrial Tribunals, which are responsible for hearing complaints of unfair dismissal, will take into account the guidance provided in the Code when considering grounds for dismissal and the procedures that the employer has followed when dismissing an employee.

It is therefore important that the Disciplinary Rules and Procedures introduced by employers follow the principles of the Code of Practice whilst being tailored to suit the requirements of their own organisation.

Why are Disciplinary Rules and Procedures necessary?

Disciplinary Rules and Procedures are necessary for a variety of reasons, for example:

- So that employees know what is expected of them in terms of standards of performance, e.g. time-keeping, quality and quantity of work, general conduct
- To make sure that all employees in different parts of the organisation are treated consistently and fairly when they become subject to disciplinary action

- To make sure that all employees know and understand the rules and procedures that will be adopted if they do not meet the required standards of performance
- To inform employees of their rights in the event that disciplinary action becomes necessary, e.g. right to be represented, right to appeal.

Preparation of Disciplinary Rules and Procedures

If there is a trade union recognised for either collective and/or individual rights then it is important for the trade union to fully support the disciplinary rules and procedures. It is usual for the disciplinary rules and procedures and grievance procedure to be incorporated into the Recognition Agreement between the company and the trade union.

If the rules and procedures are to be prepared then it is suggested that the elected trade union representatives participate in the formation of the procedures so that their full support is gained and recognised by the employees they represent.

Where there is no trade union then it is a good idea to form a committee including members of staff to act as staff representatives so that management and employees can jointly prepare the procedures.

With staff involvement there will be greater commitment to the application of the procedures and any disagreements or misunderstandings that might arise concerning the interpretation or intention of the rules and procedures can be resolved before the issues need to be tackled in practice.

When should the Disciplinary Procedures be invoked?

Except in serious cases of misconduct, e.g. theft, assault, every effort should first be made to correct the matter complained of by informal discussions prior to invoking the Disciplinary Procedure.

For example, if an employee has been arriving late for work or perhaps a number of small mistakes have been made in his/her work, the normal practice would be for the immediate supervisor to first discuss the matter informally with the employee concerned, pointing out the matters which are giving cause for complaint.

Only when this has failed to bring about the desired improvement should the formal Disciplinary Procedure be used.

Informal Discussions

As stated above, except in more serious instances, matters of concern should first be discussed informally with the employee in an attempt to resolve the matter without having to resort to formal disciplinary action.

Nine times out of ten an informal discussion in the early days of a problem having been highlighted will resolve the situation and formal disciplinary action will not be necessary. However, the longer a problem is ignored the harder it becomes for the supervisor to tackle and by ignoring the lapse in standards the supervisor is effectively giving the behaviour the "OK" by condoning it instead of pulling the employee back into line.

By pushing the problem under the carpet the situation may well deteriorate with other employees assuming they can get away with an equally poor standard of performance while others will feel demoralised because they are carrying the employees who are not pulling their weight!

Underlying causes for poor Standards of Performance

Before considering taking disciplinary action it is important to find out whether there are any underlying problems or circumstances which may be affecting the employee's behaviour and not to pre-judge the issue.

There are many factors which can affect people's performance or attitude to work and these factors and their causes need to be explored before deciding upon the path of corrective action that may be appropriate.

It may be that disciplinary action is not called for, but instead a supportive and problem-solving discussion may be more productive.

Two typical but contrasting examples are described below to demonstrate how different approaches may be appropriate even though initially the problem in each case may appear on the surface to be similar.

"Jean was employed as a Packer in a small factory which manufactured children's toys. She had been with the company for ten years and was known to be quiet, industrious and she made few mistakes.

Over the previous three weeks Jean had been late five times and when she did turn up she made a lot of silly mistakes trying to make up for the time that she had lost and because she was having difficulty concentrating on her work. When Jean arrived late, instead of speaking to her supervisor and explaining the position to her she tried instead to creep in unnoticed.

Eventually her supervisor spoke to her and was all set to launch straight into a verbal warning. On discussion with Jean it was discovered that her husband had had an accident and while he was off sick he was unable to give her a lift to work. Unfortunately, where she lived there was no bus service and Jean, who did not drive, was relying on a friend to give her a lift which meant that she was arriving late for work on occasions. In view of the short term nature of the problem it was agreed that Jean would make up any lost time by taking a shorter lunch break over the next four weeks by which time it was anticipated that her normal transport arrangements would be back in place. In this instance the possibility of Jean's poor timekeeping leading to a potential disciplinary situation was averted. Instead Jean's morale and motivation were enhanced by the supervisor's response to her genuine problem and the stress and frustration caused by her unreliable "lift" was alleviated which meant that when she did arrive her work was up to its usual high standard. She knew that these arrangements could only be tolerated for a short while otherwise the other staff in the factory would also be expecting to be allowed to make various personal arrangements. The supervisor gained by retaining an employee whose performance until now had always been exemplary and by improving staff relations generally by responding with a humane and practical solution to a genuine problem rather than blithely following the disciplinary route because an employee was unable temporarily to conform to requirements.

In this example, the underlying problem was established, the reasons found to be both genuine and short term and it was possible to agree to temporary arrangements to overcome the short term difficulty that Jean was faced with. Fortunately, Jean was able to overcome her transport difficulties within the period of time allowed and the problem was therefore solved without recourse to formal discipline."

While disciplinary action in this case was not considered to be appropriate, if the problem had continued beyond a reasonable period of time then it might have become unavoidable and the stages of the disciplinary process would have needed to be followed before the ultimate decision to dismiss was taken.

Unfortunately matters are not always so simple:

"Mike, like Jean, had until recently a good track record. He too was employed as a Packer and had been with the same company for a number of years. He had recently made friends with a new crowd of lads and was known to be enjoying a good social life with lots of late nights out at discos and clubs. Over the last month he had started to take odd days off, particularly around weekends and was frequently late getting to work in the mornings.

Mike's supervisor arranged to have an informal chat with Mike and not surprisingly Mike was unable to come up with any good explanation for the deterioration in his attendance record. The supervisor told Mike that his attendance record had become unacceptable and that it was important for him to be ready to start work at the prescribed times. Mike was advised that his attendance would continue to be monitored and that unless he pulled his socks up he could anticipate formal disciplinary action being taken.

Unfortunately Mike didn't take seriously the informal discussion with his supervisor even though he had tried to demonstrate to him that he wouldn't be able to get away with burning the candle at both ends if he wanted to keep his job and that his timekeeping must improve if formal disciplinary action was to be avoided.

Mike didn't take heed and continued to arrive late and take odd days off without a satisfactory explanation. This left the supervisor with no choice but to hold a disciplinary hearing which resulted in Mike being given an Oral Warning, i.e. the first stage in the formal disciplinary procedure."

There are many other factors which may influence an employee's behaviour or standard of performance in the workplace and these will need to be considered when determining whether disciplinary action is appropriate or whether in fact action of a totally different nature would resolve the problem, for example:

Working Relationships

Relationships either with work colleagues or management may be affecting an employee's attitude to work which in turn may result in shoddy work being undertaken or communications being handled badly.

By talking to the employee impartially and if necessary carrying out further enquiries it should be possible to establish where the problem lies and what action is appropriate to resolve the matter. It may be necessary to deal with the matter by taking it up with colleagues or members of management who may be the real cause of the problem.

Work Itself

Employees can often be reluctant to admit that they do not fully understand what is expected of them and will often muddle along without asking for further instruction or clarification for fear that they will look silly. In situations such as this it is important to consider what further training or coaching may be required and how much further time for improvement should be given to achieve standards before disciplinary action is contemplated. Even if disciplinary action does eventually become necessary, consideration should continue to be given to providing further training during the stages of the disciplinary process to give the employee every realistic opportunity of meeting the requirements.

Sometimes we expect employees to cope with work that is beyond their capabilities and then become frustrated when they cannot achieve what is required. As above, further training or coaching should be provided to assist the employee to gain the appropriate skill levels before disciplinary action is taken. If this does not resolve the issue then offering work that is more suited to the individual's abilities should be considered as an alternative to dismissal.

Work that is below the capabilities of an employee may also have disastrous side-effects in that the employee may find it difficult to maintain interest and momentum and may seek alternative ways of passing the time or making working life more interesting in ways that could be to the detriment of the workplace!

Whatever the work problem, consideration should be given to the reasons behind the poor work behaviour and whether there are problems which should be resolved by means other than a disciplinary warning.

Medical Problems

Regular attendance at work may be difficult for some employees because of genuine medical reasons.

In most cases the employer is not qualified to question the medical evidence submitted by the individual and it can often be helpful to get a second opinion either from a company medical officer or an independent medical practitioner appointed by the employer.

In any event, where there is an underlying medical problem it is important to contact the employee's own medical practitioner to find out whether the condition is likely to improve in the foreseeable future and whether the attendance record can subsequently be expected to improve. The medical practitioner should be given full details of the employee's duties so that the advice provided relates to what is required of the employee in the workplace.

For example, if an employee has problems with say his/her back then clearly a job involving lifting may be out of the question whereas a clerical job may not aggravate the person's medical problem in the long term. As well as asking for views on the employee's medical capability to continue to do his/her existing job it is also important to ask what other types of work might be considered suitable so that alternative work can be considered if the existing job is found to be medically unsuitable.

If medical opinion is sought then the agreement of the employee must first be obtained in line with the provisions of the Access to Medical Reports Act 1988. A summary of this Act is contained in Appendix One.

If there is no medical connection between the various reasons given for an individual's absence then there would be little point in seeking medical opinion. The medical practitioner would only be in a position to comment on the existing medical problem and not the various complaints which by then had presumably gone away!

An employer is not expected to tolerate an unreasonable level of poor attendance indefinitely and steps may be taken to warn the employee by following the appropriate stages of the disciplinary procedure when this point is reached.

How to cope with both short term and long term absence through ill health is dealt with more fully in Chapter Three.

What constitutes a Formal Disciplinary Procedure?

The following procedure would be appropriate when an employee fails to meet reasonable standards of performance or conduct despite the fact that informal discussions have taken place in an endeavour to correct the matters complained of.

Oral Warning

Normally, if an employee fails to meet acceptable standards of performance or conduct, the first stage in the procedure would be for an employee to be given an Oral Warning.

Prior to the decision being taken to issue an oral warning the employee should be:

■ notified of the details of the complaint before the disciplinary hearing

At the disciplinary hearing they should:

- be given the opportunity of having a representative accompany them
- be given the opportunity to state their case
- be advised of the improvement required in their standard of performance or conduct and the timescale in which these improvements must be made
- be advised of the length of time after which the warning will be disregarded
- be made aware of the procedure that will apply if they fail to make the necessary improvements, i.e. what could happen next
- be advised of their right to appeal, by when and to whom if they are not happy with the disciplinary action being taken against them

Notes of the meeting should be taken recording that an oral warning has been given and a copy kept on the individual's personnel file.

First Written Warning

If the employee continues to fail to meet the standards of performance or conduct following an oral warning, or if the complaint is more serious then a written warning may be given.

Prior to the decision being taken to issue a written warning the employee should be:

- notified in writing of the details of the complaint giving sufficient time before the disciplinary hearing is held to consider and prepare his/her response to your complaint
- given the opportunity of having a representative accompany him/her at the disciplinary hearing

At the disciplinary hearing they should:

- be given the opportunity to state his/her case
- be advised of the improvement required in his/her standard of performance or conduct and the timescale in which these improvements must be made
- be advised of the length of time after which the warning will be disregarded
- be made aware of the procedure that will apply if he/she fails to make the necessary improvements, i.e. what happens next
- be advised of his/her right to appeal, by when and to whom, if he/she is are not happy with the disciplinary action being taken against him/her.

Notes of the meeting recording the discussions should be kept on the employee's personal file. In addition the individual concerned should be given a letter summarising:

- the stage of the disciplinary procedure which has been invoked, e.g. written warning
- whether or not the individual chose to be represented and if so by whom
- a summary of the complaint(s)
- a summary of the improvements required and the timescale
- the period of time after which the warning will be disregarded
- how to appeal, by when and to whom

Final Written Warning

In the event that the employee continues to fail to meet the standards of performance or conduct required despite being given a written warning, or in the event that a complaint is considered to be very serious but that it is felt that actual dismissal is not warranted, then a final written warning may be given.

Prior to the decision being taken to issue a final written warning the employee should be:

- notified in writing giving details of the complaint giving sufficient time before the disciplinary hearing takes place to enable him/her to prepare his/her response to your complaint
- given the opportunity of having a representative accompany him/her to the disciplinary hearing

At the disciplinary hearing he/she should:

- be given the opportunity to state his/her case
- be advised of the improvement required in his/her standard of performance or conduct and the timescale in which these improvements must be made
- be advised of the length of time after which the warning will be disregarded
- be made aware of the procedure that will apply if he/she fails to make the necessary improvements, e.g. what happens next
- be advised of his/her right to appeal, by when and to whom, if he/she is not happy with the action being taken against them.

As above, notes of the meeting recording the discussions should be kept on the personnel file. In addition the individual concerned should be given a letter summarising:

- the stage of the disciplinary procedure which has been invoked, e.g. final written warning
- whether or not the individual chose to be represented and if so by whom
- a summary of the complaints

- a summary of the improvements required and the timescale
- the period of time after which the warning will be disregarded
- how to appeal, by when and to whom

Dismissal

In the event that the employee continues to fail to meet the standards of performance or conduct required despite being given a final written warning then the employee may be dismissed by being given the appropriate notice of termination of employment or, if appropriate, payment in lieu of notice.

Prior to the decision being taken to dismiss, the employee should:

- be notified in writing giving details of the complaint giving sufficient time to enable him/her to prepare his/her response to your complaint
- be given the opportunity of having a representative accompany him/her to the meeting
- be given the opportunity to state his/her case
- be advised of his/her right to appeal, by when and to whom, if he/she is not happy with the action being taken against him/her.

Following dismissal an employee who has been continuously employed for two years or more may request that he/she be provided with written reasons for his/her dismissal. This request must be made within three months of the effective date of termination and must be provided within 14 days of the request.

Even if an employee does not have sufficient service to

qualify for this right, it is good practice to provide written reasons for dismissal when requested provided that it falls within the three month timescale referred to above.

Transfer or Suspension as an Alternative to Dismissal

Where there is an express term in the contract of employment or if an employee is prepared to willingly accept a transfer to different employment then this may be considered as an alternative to dismissal. For example, an individual employed as a Branch Manager in a shop who has been finding it difficult to cope may be happy to accept demotion to the post of Senior Sales Assistant as an alternative to dismissal for lack of capability.

If there is no express term in the contract to allow such a change or if the employee refuses to accept the demotion, then the employer is left with no alternative but to dismiss, although provided the proper procedure has been followed then this would be a fair reason for dismissal. If the employer chose to impose the demotion then there would be a breach of contract.

If the employee is prepared to willingly accept the variation to his/her contract as an alternative to dismissal then this should be clearly recorded in writing and signed by both parties to ensure that the employer can demonstrate that the change was introduced with the agreement of the employee concerned and not imposed.

Another alternative to dismissal is suspension without pay. Such a penalty should not be imposed without a prior agreement existing allowing the employer to use this sanction. Without such an agreement the employer would be in breach of contract to withhold pay from an employee.

Suspension with pay is acceptable and is generally applied where further investigations are necessary before a decision is reached or for the individual's well-being or safety.

Representatives

As stated above, throughout the procedure the employee should be allowed to appoint a representative to accompany him/her. This representative may be a staff representative or a shop steward, if a trade union is recognised by the employer, or a work colleague chosen by the employee providing they are available at the time of the hearing.

As the disciplinary procedure is an internal procedure, it is not normally recommended that employees be allowed to be accompanied by an outsider such as their spouse, a personal friend or even a solicitor or individual from the Citizens Advice Bureau. To do so is likely to escalate the problem out of all proportion when the object of the exercise is to attempt to resolve the matter as speedily and as simply as possible and to enable the employee to settle back into the working environment as comfortably as possible.

In the event of a senior person becoming the subject of disciplinary action the employer should consider allowing an outsider to represent him/her if he/she does not belong to a trade union as it may be difficult to find a work colleague to undertake this role.

Whatever is decided concerning who is entitled to act as representative should be recorded in the Disciplinary Procedure so that the employees know who they are entitled to bring to any disciplinary meetings.

Determining who has authority for taking Disciplinary Action

Who is entitled to invoke disciplinary action should be clearly identified by the employer so that there are no misunderstandings either on the part of line management or their employees. Typical lines of authority are set out in Appendix One – Example Disciplinary Procedure.

Depending upon the size of organisation and the tiers of line management that exist the normal practice would be for the immediate supervisor or line manager to be responsible for dealing with matters at the informal discussion and oral warning stage.

If matters do not improve or if the matter complained of is more serious, then where they exist, disciplinary hearings should be conducted by progressively more senior levels of line management. If possible, members of management not directly involved with the matter of complaint should conduct the hearing so that a fresh mind can objectively consider the facts of the case.

Investigations

At each stage of the disciplinary procedure a full investigation of the facts available should be undertaken before any decision is reached. If necessary the meeting should be adjourned so that any mitigating circumstances which have come to light during the discussions can be checked to ensure that no stone is left unturned before deciding that disciplinary action is appropriate.

A failure to carry out a full and proper investigation could lead to an unfair dismissal.

Adjournments

Following a disciplinary hearing it is essential to have an adjournment, for however long a period may be necessary, to consider the facts before reaching a decision to invoke disciplinary action or dismissal.

Even if the matter appears to be clear cut, or there are no further points to investigate, it is important for the person who is responsible for making the decision not to pre-judge but to take time to consider the matter fully and to be able to reflect on the issues away from the environment of the meeting before reaching a decision.

The length of time needed for an adjournment may vary from as little as fifteen minutes to a number of days depending upon the complexity of the issues to be considered.

Witnesses

If appropriate, the employee who is subject to discipline should be permitted to bring to the disciplinary hearing any colleagues to act as witnesses in support of his/her actions.

Likewise, the employer may feel it appropriate to request that other employees or members of management attend the hearing to give their knowledge of the matter.

Normally, witnesses would not be required to attend the full hearing but would be present to give their input and to respond to questions only.

Depending upon the nature of the complaint, written statements by witnesses may be an acceptable alternative to attending the hearing.

Notes

As stated above it is essential that accurate and detailed notes be kept at each stage of the disciplinary process as these notes will form the basis of any evidence that may be required at an Industrial Tribunal if the employee decides to pursue a claim of Unfair Dismissal through the courts.

It is good practice to circulate the notes to all the parties attending the hearing so that their accuracy can be noted or if necessary any omissions or inaccuracies put right.

Reasons why Disciplinary Action may become necessary

Disciplinary action may become inevitable for a number of reasons. The following examples include situations which might result in the need to take disciplinary action by following the stages of the disciplinary procedure:

- Poor attendance
- Lateness
- Poor work performance, e.g. poor quality, too many mistakes made, not enough work completed, unable to achieve required number of sales
- Poor standard of housekeeping, e.g. untidy, dirty working environment
- Smoking where this is against the rules
- Refusal to obey reasonable instructions
- Behaviour which is likely to disrupt working relationships

In more serious cases of misconduct the earlier stages of discipline may be felt to be insufficient remedy for the circumstances and the following examples of gross misconduct are given where misconduct may be considered sufficiently serious as to warrant summary dismissal:

- Assault on another employee or client
- Theft
- Fraud
- Failure to take reasonable care of company property
- Disclosure of confidential information
- Disregard of health and safety requirements
- Gross negligence
- Discrimination
- Conduct prejudicial to the company's reputation

Counselling

At every stage of the procedure it is important to try to establish the underlying causes of the problem and to offer help and support where possible. Often the opportunity to talk a problem over with somebody is a problem halved in the eyes of the employee.

If the problem is outside the expertise of the supervisor or manager then where resources or facilities permit, the employee should be encouraged to take further counsel with someone who is qualified to help. This may be the Personnel Officer, Company Nurse or through the many outside bodies who provide help for various types of problems, for example Relate, Citizens Advice Bureau, Alcoholics Anonymous.

Training

As stated earlier, poor performance is often the result of an individual's having insufficient expertise or experience in coping with the standards of performance set by the organisation. It is therefore important both before formal discipline is invoked and during the disciplinary process that the provision of further training is explored with the employee concerned. This may take the form of formal external training or it may simply be a case of informal sessions designed to address the areas of concern. Whatever is agreed it should be recorded and followed up to ensure that it takes place and that the employee is given every opportunity of achieving the required standards before his/her performance is formally reviewed and further disciplinary action is contemplated.

If further training is agreed but is not followed through by no fault of the individual who is being disciplined then an ultimate decision to dismiss would very likely be seen as unfair.

If performance does not improve despite every opportunity being provided to meet the standards required then the stages of the disciplinary process should be followed.

Follow up actions

At each stage of the disciplinary procedure the standards of performance which are desired should be discussed and realistic goals set with the commitment of the employee to attempt to meet those goals.

A date should be mutually agreed when performance will be reviewed so that progress can be discussed with the employee. The effectiveness of any training or coaching provided should be discussed and assessed and any further difficulties in achieving standards raised to see what further assistance may be provided.

When performance has reached an acceptable standard then the employee should be advised of this in writing, whilst also reminding him/her of the period of time during which the warning will remain on file before it is disregarded.

Duration of warnings

Disciplinary warnings will normally be disregarded after a certain period of time has elapsed.

The length of time that warnings remain on the employee's file will depend on the seriousness of the offence and the stage at which disciplinary action has been instigated.

The following timescales may be used as a guide:

- Oral Warning   Six months
- First Written Warning   One year
- Final Written Warning   Two Years

There are occasionally circumstances where the misconduct is so serious, verging on gross misconduct, where it could not be disregarded in the future. In these situations it should be clearly stated in the letter recording the disciplinary action that the final warning will never be disregarded and that any recurrence of the matter complained of will lead to dismissal.

Examples of such situations might include

- sex or race discrimination where the matter complained of fell short of warranting dismissal
- theft, but it was felt that there were mitigating circumstances
- abusive or violent behaviour, but it was felt that there was some provocation

Training in Disciplinary Procedures

It is essential that all those who may be responsible for instigating the disciplinary rules and procedures, i.e. all those who have responsibility for staff, be fully trained so that they understand:

- what is actually meant by discipline
- when disciplinary action should be applied
- what level of authority they have in administering discipline
- how the rules should be applied
- what issues the organisation recognises as warranting disciplinary action both under the headings of ordinary and gross misconduct as well as issues of performance
- what resources are available to them for advice, e.g. Personnel Department or a designated senior manager

Disciplinary Appeals

Requirement to provide a Disciplinary Appeals Procedure

Employees are entitled by law to appeal if they consider that the disciplinary action taken against them is unreasonable.

The person or job title to whom they should appeal or the procedure which they are required to follow should be set out in their written Statement of Main Terms and Conditions of Employment or the Contract of Employment. This information should be included in the Disciplinary Procedure where this is supplied.

Why is a Disciplinary Appeals Procedure necessary?

A disciplinary procedure is necessary to ensure that:

■ there is a recognised means whereby employees can appeal if they consider that the action taken against them is unreasonable

■ if challenged, disciplinary action taken can be independently assessed by a higher level of management, where possible, and subsequently endorsed or rescinded as may be considered appropriate

■ management use their authority to apply discipline in genuine circumstances and in a fair and consistent manner.

What constitutes a Formal Disciplinary Appeals Procedure?

The principles of the Disciplinary Appeals Procedure will be similar to the Grievance Procedure described in Chapter Two – Grievance, except that wherever possible the appeal should be made to a person more senior than the one who administered the disciplinary action.

In small organisations this may not be possible in which case the same person will have to hear the appeal. It is therefore advisable to hold the appeal interview a short while after the disciplinary action has been taken to allow time for both sides to reflect on the matter and perhaps be more objective.

As with the grievance procedure, employees should be advised of the time limit in which to appeal against disciplinary action, to whom the appeal should be addressed and that they have the right to be represented if they wish. It is advisable to include this information in the letter to the employee which confirms the details of the disciplinary action that has been taken.

Failure to allow an Employee to Appeal against Disciplinary Action

If an employee is denied the opportunity to appeal against disciplinary action that has been taken against him/her and subsequently the individual submits a claim to an Industrial Tribunal for unfair dismissal, the claim will more than likely be found in favour of the employee.

Even though the reasons for the dismissal may have been fair, the fact that the procedure has not been followed may be sufficient grounds to uphold the complaint.

2 Grievance

Requirement to provide a Grievance Procedure

Any employee who considers that he/she have a grievance in relation to his/her employment is entitled by law to raise the matter through a grievance procedure.

All employers are required to include in the Written Statement of Main Terms and Conditions of Employment or the Contract of Employment which they issue to their employees, either the name or job title of the person to whom they should apply if they wish to raise a grievance or alternatively details of the Grievance Procedure which is applicable to them.

Typical issues which may be raised through the grievance procedure may include:

- Dissatisfaction with actual pay or benefits
- Dissatisfaction with working arrangements

- Unhappy with working relationships
- Unhappy with career progression
- Disagreement with job evaluation grading
- Complaints about other members of staff

Why is a Grievance Procedure necessary?

A grievance procedure is necessary for a variety of reasons, for example:

- To inform employees of their rights in the event that they have a complaint concerning matters connected with their employment
- To ensure that matters of disagreement are resolved as quickly as possible
- To ensure that all employees in the organisation are treated fairly and consistently if they wish to raise a complaint
- To provide a means whereby an employee can raise a complaint at various levels of the organisation's hierarchy if he/she fails to get satisfaction with his/her immediate line management

The grievance procedure is not intended to take away the responsibility of line management or the supervisor whose role is to discuss and attempt to resolve problems that occur. Instead the grievance procedure should only be used when these attempts fail.

When should the Grievance Procedure be used?

Informal Discussions

An employee should attempt to resolve ordinary, day-to-day issues by informal discussion with his/her immediate supervisor or line manager. Only when this has failed to bring about a satisfactory solution or if the matter is considered to be more serious, should the matter be raised formally through the grievance procedure.

Time Limit

The grievance procedure should state a time limit within which employees who have a grievance should raise their complaint. Typically grievance procedures allow 5 or 10 working days in which to lodge a grievance following the matter occurring which has given cause for complaint.

What constitutes a Formal Grievance Procedure?

A grievance procedure sets out the stages which an employee must follow if he/she wishes to raise a complaint concerning matters affecting his/her employment. The number of stages will depend upon the size of organisation and the tiers of management that exist. In small organisations the employee may have only the owner of the business to whom to take his/her complaint. Whatever the size of organisation, however many the tiers of management, the procedure should allow for the employee's complaint to be heard as objectively and fairly as possible.

Some organisations may choose to involve a mutually

acceptable independent arbitrator as the final stage in their grievance procedure.

The following principles demonstrate the stages of a typical grievance procedure:

Stage One

Normally in the first instance the employee should raise his/her complaint with his/her supervisor or immediate line manager. Ideally this should be in writing, giving brief details of the matter complained of.

A meeting should be held with the employee concerned within the next few days to enable the employee to explain fully the matters giving him/her cause for concern.

If he/she wishes, the employee is entitled to bring to the meeting his/her staff representative or shop steward, if there is a recognised trade union, or a work colleague of his/her choice.

Notes should be made of the meeting, a copy given to the employee and a copy held on the employee's personal file.

Every effort should be made by both parties to resolve the matter as speedily as possible.

Stage Two

If the matter is not resolved to the satisfaction of the employee within a reasonable period of time, then the employee is entitled to raise his/her complaint with the next level of management. Again, this should be requested in writing, giving brief details of the matter complained of.

A meeting should be held between this level of management and the employee within the next few days to enable the employee to again explain fully the matters giving cause for concern.

If he/she wishes, the employee is entitled to bring to the meeting his/her staff representative or shop steward if there is a recognised trade union, or a work colleague of their choice.

Notes should be made of the meeting, a copy given to the employee and a copy held on the employee's personal file.

Every effort should be made by both parties to resolve the matter as speedily as possible.

Stage Three

If the matter is still unresolved to the satisfaction of the employee within a reasonable period of time then the employee is entitled to raise his/her complaint with the next level of management whose decision will be final. This should again be requested in writing, giving brief details of the matter complained of.

As described above a meeting should be arranged as soon as possible to enable the employee to put his/her case forward.

If he/she wishes, the employee is entitled to bring to the meeting his/her staff representative or shop steward if there is a recognised trade union, or a work colleague of his/her choice.

Notes should be made of the meeting, a copy given to the employee and a copy held on the employee's personal file.

Every effort should be made by both parties to resolve the matter as speedily as possible.

Notes

As with notes of disciplinary hearings, it is important that accurate and detailed notes are kept at each stage of the grievance procedure. If at a later date the employee decides to leave as a result of his/her grievance not being resolved then the notes of the meetings will form the basis of the documentary evidence that will be required if the employee brings a claim of Constructive Dismissal at the Industrial Tribunal.

It is recommended that notes are circulated to all parties present at the grievance interview so that their accuracy can be recorded or any omissions or inaccuracies put right.

Fairness and Consistency in handling a Grievance

To ensure that employees are dealt with fairly and consistently when pursuing the grievance procedure, the following points should be borne in mind

1 A chance to explain

At each stage of the grievance procedure the employee should be given every opportunity to state his/her case fully without fear of repercussions or recriminations from management

2 Investigate

The member of management hearing the grievance should ensure that any investigations that may be appropriate are fully undertaken to ensure that all the facts are brought to light

3 **Right to be represented**

As stated above the employee is entitled to bring to the meetings a representative of his/her choice. If there is a staff association or a recognised trade union then this person may be his/her staff representative or shop steward. Where there is no staff representation then a work colleague who is available at the required time may be allowed to attend.

As with the disciplinary procedure, some organisations allow the representative to be from outside the organisation, e.g. spouse, solicitor or the Citizens Advice Bureau. It is suggested that the written Grievance Procedure specify who the employee is entitled to ask to represent him/her to avoid misunderstandings.

4 Who should hear the Grievance

The first stage in the grievance procedure will normally be the employee's immediate line management.

The second stage would normally be the next level of management up from the employee's immediate line management.

The third stage of the procedure will normally be the next highest level of management. In some organisations this may be the Managing Director or it may be a panel of senior managers or directors who were not involved in hearing the earlier stages of the grievance.

As stated above, some organisations may build into the final stage of their procedure the right to use a mutually acceptable arbitrator such as ACAS or some other mutually agreed individual. If this is the case then it should be agreed beforehand whether or not the independent arbitrator's decision will be binding.

Failure to respond to a Grievance

If an employee is denied the opportunity of having his/her grievance heard through the grievance procedure and subsequently the individual submits a claim to the Industrial Tribunal for constructive dismissal, the claim will more than likely be found in favour of the employee.

Even though the employee's claim that he/she was constructively dismissed may be without substance, if the organisation made no attempt to resolve the complaint by allowing the grievance to be heard then the case may fail on procedural grounds.

Grievances concerning Harassment

Following the EC Directive concerning the protection of the dignity of men and women at work all organisations are required to have a procedure for dealing specifically with complaints of harassment.

Definition of Harassment

It is for each individual to determine what behaviour they find offensive and what they find acceptable. If the behaviour is unwanted then it will be regarded as harassment whereas if the recipient finds the behaviour welcome then clearly it will be regarded as friendly and wanted.

Harassment occurs when one person's or a group of people's behaviour towards another gives cause for offence. Behaviour may be by a person of one sex to a person of the same or opposite sex or of one racial group to a person of the same or another racial group.

Examples of Harassment

- Embarrassing remarks
- Jokes
- Insults
- Ridicule
- Comments about appearance, facial or other physical expressions
- Physical contact
- Suggestions or demands for sexual favours
- Displays of suggestive photographs or pictures
- Racial shunning or segregation
- Racial abuse

History

It has become apparent that while harassment on grounds of either sex or race is nothing new it has not been taken seriously by employers.

For example junior staff may have felt too frightened to complain particularly if their only contact with management has been the person who is harassing them!

In other instances the harassment may have been regarded as harmless fun regardless of the hurt or embarrassment that was being caused to the target employee.

A typical example of this is the case of Johnstone v Fenton Barns (Scotland) Ltd where Ms Johnstone complained of the lewd behaviour of her colleagues. Her employer ignored her complaints as he felt that the behaviour complained of was not unusual in the context of the factory environment that Ms Johnstone was employed in and that none of the incidents complained of had been specifically directed at her. The lewd behaviour continued and eventually Ms Johnstone submitted a claim for sexual harassment to the Industrial Tribunal. Her claim was upheld under the concept of discrimination and she was awarded a compensatory award including injury to feelings.

Why is a separate Complaints Procedure for Harassment necessary?

A procedure separate from the normal grievance procedure is necessary for a variety of reasons, for example:

■ an employee may feel unable to pursue a complaint through the normal grievance procedure if the complaint is of a sensitive personal nature and/or the immediate line management is a member of the opposite sex

■ the harasser may be the employee's immediate supervisor or the next level of management which means that under the normal grievance procedure they would be the individuals to whom the harassed would be required to take his/her grievance

■ the opportunity should be provided for any investigation that may be warranted to be undertaken by a suitable designated person where this would be more appropriate

■ the complaint, if found to be justified, could lead to disciplinary action being taken against another employee therefore the complainant may be required to provide evidence to a disciplinary hearing.

When should the separate Complaints Procedure be used?

Time Limit

As with the normal grievance procedure, the complaints procedure should provide a time limit within which the employee should raise his/her complaint with the harasser. Following similar principles to the grievance procedure it is suggested that 5 or 10 days be allowed in which to lodge a complaint following the matter occurring.

Informal Discussions

Depending upon the seriousness of the harassment, the employee would, in the first instance, be expected to speak to the harasser personally and make it clear that the behaviour is unwanted.

If the employee finds that the matter is too embarrassing or that it is too difficult for him/her to do this personally then he/she may ask his/her representative to do this on his/her behalf.

The employee should keep a note of these discussions, as should the harasser.

What constitutes a Formal Complaints Procedure?

Formal complaint

If an informal approach to the harasser fails to resolve the issue or the matter complained of is of a more serious nature, then the employee should speak directly to his/her supervisor or immediate line management. If the matter is too embarrassing then the matter may be raised with any other member of management. For example, an employee may prefer to talk to a member of the same sex or ethnic origin.

The employee concerned may be required to confirm the complaint in writing, giving details of the matters giving cause for concern together with details of any previous discussions in which he/she told the harasser that the behaviour was unwanted.

If the employee finds that it is too difficult to do this then he/she should be permitted to ask his/her representative to act on their behalf.

Disciplinary Action

If the matter complained of results in another employee being involved in a disciplinary hearing then the complainant may be required to provide evidence for the hearing. The complainant's representative may be present at the hearing if requested by the employee who has lodged the complaint but would not normally be permitted to participate unless specifically approached.

The action taken against the harasser will depend upon the severity and/or persistency of the offence. A minor offence for example could result in an oral warning being given whereas a very serious offence could result in summary dismissal.

Consideration may be given to moving the harasser's place of work away from the harassed. Alternatively, or where it is not possible to move the harasser, the person harassed may be offered the opportunity to be transferred elsewhere within the organisation.

It may also be appropriate to consider whether counselling from an appropriate outside body may be offered to the harasser to enable him/her to overcome his/her problems.

Right of Appeal for Harasser

The harasser should have the right to appeal against the disciplinary action taken by following the normal procedure for disciplinary appeals.

Outcome

The employee who has raised the complaint should be notified, in writing, of the outcome of his/her complaint and what action, if any, has been taken.

If an employee considers that he/she has been victimised as a result of raising a complaint of harassment then he/she may submit a claim to the Industrial Tribunal under the

Race Relations Act 1976 or Sex Discrimination Act 1975 (as amended).

Representatives

As with the normal grievance procedure, the employee should be allowed to appoint a representative to accompany him/her at all stages of the procedure. This representative may be a staff representative or a shop steward where there is a trade union recognised, or a work colleague of his/her choice who is available at the time of the meeting.

As the procedure is an internal procedure it is not recommended that employees be allowed to be accompanied by an outsider such as a solicitor or the Citizens Advice Bureau. However in view of the sensitive nature of this procedure it may be felt appropriate to allow a personal friend who is not a work colleague or a member of the employee's family to attend.

Whatever is decided, concerning who may be entitled to represent the employee, should be recorded in the procedure to avoid misunderstandings or disagreement at a later date.

Notes

It is essential that accurate and detailed notes be kept at each stage of the procedure. If the employee who is being harassed brings a claim of Discrimination to the Industrial Tribunal or if the harasser is dismissed then these notes will form the basis of the evidence upon which the organisation may wish to rely at the Tribunal Hearing.

It is advisable to circulate the notes, on a strictly confidential basis, to those present at the meetings so that their accuracy can be confirmed or any omissions or inaccuracies put right.

Confidentiality

It is essential that all those involved in a complaint of harassment treat the matter with the highest degree of confidentiality in view of the potentially highly sensitive nature of the complaint.

Any breaches of this confidentiality should be dealt with through the disciplinary process.

Failure to follow up an Employee's Complaint of Harassment

If an employee lodges a complaint of harassment and it is ignored, then a claim may be brought by the employee to Industrial Tribunal against both the employer and the harasser.

If the claim is found to be justified then a compensatory award (for the year 1992/93 this may be up to £10,000) may be made including an element for injured feelings. A proportion of this award may be directed at the harasser although it will be for the organisation to decide if it is willing to foot the whole bill or require the harasser to be responsible for that proportion.

As stated earlier there is no requirement for an employee to accrue any period of continuous service to bring a claim of either Sex or Race Discrimination

Disciplinary Appeals

Although the principles of the Disciplinary Appeals Procedure will be similar to the Grievance Procedure described above there should be a separate procedure so that wherever possible the appeal is be made to a person more senior than the one who administered the disciplinary action. Disciplinary Appeals are discussed in Chapter One – Discipline.

3

Dismissal

Protection from Unfair Dismissal

Employees who are under their company's normal retirement age and have two years' continuous service working 16 hours or more per week (or have five years' continuous service working 8 hours but less than 16 hours per week) are given legal protection against being dismissed unfairly.

There is no qualifying period for claims of unfair dismissal arising from trade union membership, non-membership of a trade union, sex or race discrimination.

Fair Dismissals

There are certain reasons where dismissal is potentially "fair" provided that the employer acts "reasonably" throughout the dismissal process and the reason was sufficient to justify dismissal. These reasons are:

1 Capability
2 Conduct
3 Redundancy
4 Contravention of some statutory requirement
5 Some other substantial reason

If a claim of unfair dismissal is submitted to the Industrial Tribunal it is up to the employer to establish the reason for the dismissal and the Industrial Tribunal will then decide if the employer acted reasonably or unreasonably in treating the reason for the dismissal as sufficient, taking into account the size and resources of the organisation.

The Industrial Tribunal will consider whether the employer's decision to dismiss fell within the band of reasonable responses to the employee's conduct which a reasonable employer would adopt.

Capability

Dismissal relating to an employee's capability could relate either to their lack of ability to do their job or their incapability to do their job because of their ill health.

Lack of ability to do the job

Before an employee is dismissed because of his/her lack of ability to do the job the following steps should be taken:

1 **Informal discussions**

   The employee should be advised informally of their shortcomings and the standards of performance that are required of them.

2 Disciplinary warnings

If the employee fails to correct the behaviour complained of then the Disciplinary Procedure should be followed, e.g. Oral warning, Written Warning, Final Written Warning prior to Dismissal.

3 A chance to explain

At each stage of the disciplinary process the employee should be given the opportunity of putting his/her side of the situation to his/her employer so that any extenuating circumstances can be fully taken into account before any disciplinary action is decided upon.

4 Time to improve

A reasonable time should be agreed with the employee for the necessary improvements to be made and maintained.

The timescales agreed for a review of performance will depend on the nature of the complaint but the time must be realistic and sufficiently long for realistic improvements to be achievable.

5 Help with achieving improvement

Advice should be given to the employee on how the necessary improvements can be achieved. If appropriate training or coaching should be provided.

6 Appeal

The employee should be made aware of the procedure to follow if he/she is dissatisfied with the action being taken against him/her. He/she should be told how and when the appeal should be made and to whom.

The above stages of the Disciplinary Procedure are described more fully in Chapter One.

Incapability as a result of Ill Health

An employee who is continually absent from work due to ill health may be fairly dismissed provided that fair and reasonable steps are followed.

Long Term Absence due to Ill Health

When an employee is off sick for prolonged periods at a time it is important for the employer to maintain contact, not just from the point of view of keeping the employee in touch with the workplace and feeling "wanted and part of the team" but also so that the employer can keep the employee aware of what is in the mind of the employer concerning the absence. The following is a guide to the steps that should be followed:

1 **Consult the employee**

   If absence continues and the employer considers that the job cannot continue to be held open indefinitely then the employee should first of all be consulted and advised that the organisation must consider the needs of the business against any foreseeable return or otherwise of the employee.

2 **Obtain a medical report**

   Even if the employee is able to give what appears to be an up to date picture of his/her health situation it is important for the employer to obtain a medical report from the employee's medical practitioner so that the facts can be investigated fully.

In asking for a medical report, the employee must first be advised of his/her rights under the Access to Medical Reports Act 1988 and give his/her written consent to a report's being obtained. A summary of the Act is contained in Appendix Four.

If the employee refuses to allow a report to be obtained then he/she should be advised that to refuse will mean that a decision will have to be made in the absence of this information which may or may not be to his/her advantage.

3 Balance medical report against business needs

Having obtained the medical report it will be possible to assess if and how soon it is hoped that the individual will be able to return to work. This will enable the organisation to decide whether or not they can continue to wait for the employee to return, taking into account the nature of the work undertaken and the difficulties caused by the employee's absence.

In Spencer v Paragon Wallpapers EAT, Mr Spencer had been off sick with a bad back for two months during a period when for operational reasons the company needed every available person to be at work. Mr Spencer's general practitioner was asked for a medical report and advised that Mr Spencer would not be fit to return for at least another four to six weeks. Paragon Wallpapers felt that because of their operational needs they were unable to wait that length of time for Mr Spencer to return and took the decision to dismiss.

The dismissal was found to be fair: the employer had considered the nature of the illness and the likely period of absence having obtained a doctor's report, they had consulted with Mr Spencer and the view that they could not be expected to wait any longer was considered reasonable under the circumstances.

This case demonstrates that while it would be reasonable to expect an employer to wait for a lengthy period for the return of an employee engaged in highly individual, specialised work due to the difficulty of providing cover, it would be another story if the work could easily be covered by others within the same department or by the ready availability of temporary workers skilled in the same tasks.

4 **Consider whether there is suitable alternative work**

If the medical practitioner recommends that the employee should not return to his/her normal duties then suitable alternative work should be considered. The employer is not obliged to create a new post but if work is available that is considered to be suitable then the employee should be given the opportunity of transferring to a position which is suited to his/her capabilities.

If, after having followed the above steps,
- the employee is unable to return to work within a reasonable period of time or
- where the medical practitioner has stated that there is no likelihood of a return to work in the foreseeable future
- or that the occupation followed is unsuitable for the employee's medical condition and no alternative work is available
- then dismissal on the grounds of the employee's incapability will be seen to be fair.

Short Term Absences due to Ill Health

It can often be more difficult for an employer to deal with a situation where an employee has a series of short term absences which are due to genuine health reasons but are nevertheless causing disruption to the running of the business.

The first point to establish is whether or not the absences are due to related reasons.

Unrelated Short Term Absences

If the reasons for an employee's absences appear to be unrelated, e.g. cold, backache, upset stomach, twisted ankle, then clearly there is no underlying connection and there would be little point seeking a medical report. If a medical report were obtained, the medical practitioner would only be able to give opinion on the complaint that existed at the time as the earlier problems would most probably have been long gone!

One of the leading cases which highlights this type of situation is International Sports Company v Thompson 1980. Mrs Thompson had a significantly higher level of absenteeism than the level considered acceptable by her company. She had received a series of warnings regarding her level of absenteeism with little effect and eventually the Company Doctor was consulted. His view was that no useful purpose would be served by seeing Mrs Thompson as there appeared to be no common link between the illnesses which had been certified as "dizzy spells, anxiety and nerves, bronchitis, virus infection, cystitis, dyspepsia and flatulence". The Industrial Tribunal found the dismissal unfair but the company appealed and the EAT reversed the decision on the basis that a fair review of the absences had taken place and the appropriate warnings had been given.

Under these circumstances then, the steps to follow would be based on the principles of the disciplinary procedure when dealing with matters of conduct and are as summarised below:

1 **Informal discussions with the employee**

Advise the employee that his/her level of attendance is unacceptable and that the needs of the business must be considered against his/her ability to attend for work.

He/she should be advised of the standard of attendance that is expected of him/her and a comparison drawn with levels of attendance within the organisation so that the employee concerned can see that he/she is out of line.

2 **Disciplinary warnings**

If the employee fails to make significant improvements in his/her attendance record then the Disciplinary Procedure should be followed, e.g. Oral Warning, Written Warning, Final Written Warning prior to Dismissal.

3 **A chance to explain**

At each stage of the disciplinary process the employee should be given the opportunity of putting to the employer his/her side of the situation so that all circumstances can be considered before any disciplinary action is decided upon.

4 **Review of attendance**

A reasonable time should be agreed with the employee following which the level of attendance should be assessed for improvement.

5 **Help with achieving improvement**

Advice should be offered to the employee on how the necessary improvements can be achieved.

If appropriate a visit to the Company medical officer or nurse should be offered, or the offer of counselling from professional sources may be more suitable.

6 **Alternative work**

If appropriate, discuss with the employee whether alternative work, if available, might help the employee achieve the necessary standard of performance.

7 **Appeal**

As with all stages of the disciplinary process the employee should be reminded of the right to appeal, how and when the appeal should be made and to whom.

If, after having followed the above steps the employee's attendance record does not improve to an acceptable level when compared with other employees and their circumstances within the organisation, then dismissal on the grounds of their unsatisfactory level of absenteeism will be considered fair.

Conduct

Examples of "ordinary" conduct that may warrant disciplinary action and subsequently dismissal are set out in Chapter One.

A dismissal following the disciplinary process will result in termination of employment by giving the period of notice of termination of employment to which the employee is entitled or with payment in lieu of notice.

To ensure that the decision to dismiss is taken fairly and reasonably the following points should be adhered to:

1 Warnings

Except in the case of gross misconduct employees should be given at least one written disciplinary warning prior to being dismissed. Full details of the disciplinary process are set out in Chapter One.

2 Consistency

The essence of a good disciplinary procedure is to ensure that employees are treated fairly and consistently whilst taking into account the individual circumstances of each situation carefully.

Even where warnings have been given in line with the disciplinary procedure the dismissal may be deemed to be unfair if other employees have been treated more leniently in similar circumstances.

3 Right to state case

Before a decision is reached as to whether discipline and/or ultimately dismissal is appropriate the employee should be given every opportunity to put his/her side of the case.

Depending on the nature of the offence the employee should be advised in advance of the details of the complaint and be given sufficient time before the interview takes place so that he/she may prepare for the interview.

If necessary the disciplinary hearing should be adjourned so that any mitigating circumstances put forward by the employee may be fully checked out and considered prior to a decision being reached.

4 Right to be represented

All employees have the right to bring a representative to the disciplinary hearings at any stage of the procedure.

If there is a staff association or if a trade union is recognised by the employer for the purpose of representing specific grades of staff then the employee is entitled to bring along his/her staff representative or shop steward.

If there is no formal representation then the employee may bring a work colleague to the meetings.

Some organisations allow the representative to be from outside the organisation, e.g. spouse, solicitor or the Citizens Advice Bureau. It is suggested that the written Disciplinary Rules and Procedures specify who the employee is entitled to ask to represent him/her so that misunderstandings do not occur in the heat of the moment.

If the employer refuses to allow a representative to be present then even though the reasons for the dismissal may be seen to be fair the actual procedure that was followed, i.e. in not allowing representation, will undoubtedly be seen to be unfair.

5 Right to appeal

Throughout the disciplinary process and following dismissal the employee has the right to appeal.

The employee should be advised of the Appeals

Procedure including who he/she should appeal to, whether it should be in writing and what time limit applies.

Wherever possible, the appeal should be made to a higher level of management than the person who took the decision to discipline and/or dismiss.

If this is not possible due to the size of the organisation then the same person may hear the appeal but it is advisable to leave a short period of time between dismissal and appeal hearing so that emotions have a chance to settle enabling the appeal to be heard as objectively as possible. Some small organisations may, with the mutual agreement of the employee, arrange for an independent, unbiased arbitrator to hear the appeal such as ACAS (Advisory, Conciliation and Arbitration Service).

The appeal should be heard and the outcome conveyed to the employee as soon as practicable.

Gross Misconduct

Examples of what constitutes "gross" misconduct are set out in Chapter One.

Where an act of gross misconduct occurs an employee may be dismissed for a first offence, without warning and without payment in lieu of notice.

The steps that should be followed to ensure that the dismissal is handled fairly and reasonably are as described above for dealing with complaints of conduct, i.e.:

1 Warnings

If the matter complained of is sufficiently serious as to be regarded as gross misconduct then it is not necessary

for there to have been a prior warning concerning the misconduct.

2 Consistency

It is important that all employees are treated fairly and consistently whilst taking each individual's circumstances into account when determining whether the misconduct complained of is serious enough to be deemed to be gross misconduct.

3 Right to state case

Before a decision is reached as to whether summary dismissal is appropriate the employee should be given every opportunity to put his/her side of the case.

Depending upon the nature of the offence the employee should be advised in advance of the details of the complaint and be given sufficient time before the interview takes place so that he/she may prepare for the interview.

If necessary the disciplinary hearing should be adjourned so that any mitigating circumstances put forward by the employee may be fully checked and considered prior to a decision being reached.

4 Right to be represented

As stated above all employees have the right to bring a representative to the disciplinary hearings.

5 Right to appeal

As stated above the employee has the right to appeal following dismissal

Suspension

It may be considered that there are matters requiring investigation before the disciplinary hearing can be arranged but that it would be inappropriate for the employee to remain at work during this period.

Under these circumstances the employee may be suspended on full pay while the necessary investigations are carried out. For the sake of both the employee and the company, the investigations should be undertaken as speedily as practicable so that the matter can be resolved without undue delay.

Particular problems when dealing with Dismissals for Misconduct

In cases of dismissal for misconduct it is for the employer to show that the reason for the dismissal was for misconduct and that he/she had acted reasonably in dismissing for that reason. By acting reasonably the employer must investigate the misconduct fully and fairly and allow the employee to put his/her side of the case in explanation or mitigation before a decision is reached. The above principles were laid down by the House of Lords in Polkey v A E Dayton Services Ltd 1987. Disregard of these principles will make a potentially fair dismissal unfair through the failure to follow a reasonable procedure.

Off duty conduct

Normally, what employees do in their own free time is of no consequence to their employer unless their off duty conduct has an adverse affect on their relationship with their employer in which case the dismissal may be seen to be fair.

For example, if:

- the adverse publicity concerning the employee may have a detrimental effect on the employer's business as a result of his/her behaviour
- the friction created between the employee and his/her colleagues is such that to continue working together has become impossible
- the relationship of trust and confidence has irretrievably broken down between employer and employee
- the employee is involved in activities outside work which

could make him/her unsuitable for the job, e.g. working in competition with his/her employer

Criminal offences

If an employee commits a criminal offence at work, the employer is not bound to wait for a conviction before dismissing the employee for gross misconduct. Providing the employer has carried out a full and proper investigation and has a genuine belief on reasonable grounds that the employee has committed the offence then the dismissal will be seen to be fair.

Criminal offences and convictions that occur outside the workplace are referred to under "Some other Substantial Reason" for dismissal.

Imprisonment

Imprisonment in itself is not sufficient grounds to dismiss an employee. Leaving aside the reasons for the imprisonment, whether or not it is fair to dismiss will depend on factors such as the likely duration of the sentence, whether an appeal is likely to be successsful, the nature of the employee's work and status within the organisation.

As with all absences, the length of the likely absence must be considered in the light of how long a reasonable employer can be expected to wait. This will depend on the exclusivity of the employee's job, whether or not a temporary replacement could be readily found and the effect that the absence is having on business operations. Also, the more senior the employee the greater is the likelihood of the organisation's reputation being tarnished and the employee's credibility and effectiveness with clients or even his/her own colleagues being likely to be impaired.

Dishonesty

It is not always possible to prove that an individual has committed a particular offence if, for example, goods or money have been stolen. However, as established by British Home Stores Ltd v Burchell EAT 1978, if following full and thorough investigation the employer believes that a particular individual is guilty of the offence and has reasonable grounds on which to base that belief then dismissal will be deemed to be fair. Unlike the criminal courts where it must be established beyond reasonable doubt that the employee is guilty, British Home Stores Ltd v Burchell lays down the principle that the employer only has to establish a genuine belief in the misconduct on the balance of probabilities for the dismissal to be treated as fair.

In contrast to British Home Stores v Burchell, where an employer is unable to determine which employee or employees have committed an offence then provided that the employer has done everything possible to narrow the field by full and thorough investigation it will be fair to dismiss all those employees under suspicion.

This situation is explained by the leading case of Monie v Coral Racing Ltd CA 1981 where two people were suspected of misconduct and the employer could not establish which one was to blame and that it could only have been one or other or both of the employees together who had committed the offence, despite carrying out full and proper investigation. It was found to be fair to dismiss both employees on reasonable suspicion short of actual belief.

Whether it is fair to dismiss for dishonesty which is

unconnected with the workplace will depend to what extent the employer's business is at risk because of the offender's job, the nature of the business, whether it is likely to affect the employer's reputation and the status of the employee within the organisation. Generally the more senior the employee then the more likely is the dismissal to be considered fair.

In Rosbotham v Foster Motors Ltd COIT, Mr Rosbotham was a 17 year-old apprentice who was fined following a drinking spree when he broke into a car and stole some goods. In this case dismissal was considered by the Industrial Tribunal to be too severe particularly bearing in mind that he was a young trainee with a specified time in which to complete his apprenticeship.

At the other end of the scale, in Rowan v GLC COIT, Mr Rowan was a senior psychologist who was convicted of a well-organised system of fare dodging on London Transport. The Industrial Tribunal considered that in view of his seniority the distinction between whether the dishonesty occurred at work or outside work made little difference and the dismissal was upheld as fair.

Fighting
Providing there is a link with the working relationship then off-duty fighting may be seen to be fair grounds for dismissal. The fairness of the dismissal will also depend on factors such as the status of the employee, whether other employees feel threatened, whether the organisation's image is likely to be affected and how closely related the incident is to the workplace. Fighting following company social functions, particularly at Christmas, are classic times when such problems occur.

In Sonoco Capseals Liners Ltd v Keshwala EAT Mr Keshwala was involved in two fights out of working hours, one of which was in the company car park. EAT held that dismissal was fair because the incidents were clearly work related and that as the company was small the repercussions were potentially dangerous and counter-productive to working relationships.

Sexual offences

Fairness of dismissal of an employee convicted of sexual offences outside the workplace would depend upon the connection between the offence and the employment. For example, the nature of the employee's job, the objections of other employees.

In Saunders v Scottish National Camps Association Ltd 1981 Court of Session, Mr Saunders was employed as a handyman. He was later found to be homosexual and to have been involved in a homosexual incident. His employers dismissed him when they found out because they felt he was unsuitable to be employed at a camp accommodating large numbers of school children and teenagers. It was considered that a considerable proportion of employers would take the view that employment of a homosexual should be restricted particularly when working in close proximity with children and that the employer's decision to dismiss as the only safe course of action to take was reasonable.

In Greenaway v Blue Circle Industries plc COIT, Mr Greenaway had over 20 years' service when he was sentenced to prison for indecently assaulting his step daughter. His employers had originally planned to re-employ him but changed their mind when it was discovered that one of the offences took place on the company's premises. The Industrial Tribunal found that the dismissal was fair because the employer was concerned that the new information which had been discovered would have brought the company's name into disrepute and would have embarrassed his colleagues.

Moonlighting

Employers will often have a written term in their contract of employment expressly stating that their employees may not take up any other employment in their spare time without the express permission of the employer. Without such a term in the contract, the courts are generally reluctant to find dismissals fair for moonlighting unless the employer's business is likely to be adversely affected. However, in determining what is reasonable the Industrial Tribunal will consider the status of the employee, the hours worked, the nature of the business, the type of work undertaken and whether there is a conflict of interest.

If an employee works for another company in his spare time or even works on a freelance basis, if the employer is genuinely concerned that this action may be in conflict with the interests of his own business or if there is an express term in the contract then this may be seen to be a fair dismissal.

For example, in Nova Plastics Ltd v Froggatt EAT 1982, Mr Froggatt worked as an odd job man for a rival company in his spare time. His dismissal was found to be unfair because his duties for the rival company did not have an adverse effect on his main employer and there was therefore no breach of trust because he worked for a competitor in his spare time.

In contrast, in Casson v John Lewis & Co EAT Ms Casson did not comply with the requirement to advise her employers of her outside activities and, when she was found out, lied about her involvement. Her dismissal was found to be fair even though her other activities were unconnected with her main employment.

Failing to return from holiday on the agreed date

Increasingly employers are allowing their employees to take extended holidays either with or without pay, often to visit relatives who live abroad. There is no statutory right to such leave.

If an employee fails to return by the agreed date then this should be treated as any other failure to abide by the organisation's rules and procedures and the matter should be investigated as fully as possible before deciding upon the appropriate disciplinary action to be taken.

Before deciding to dismiss, the employee's age, service, reliability and explanation should be fully considered.

Failing to return to work

Occasionally employees fail to return to work without contacting the organisation with an explanation. It may be that they are sick or have simply decided not to return to their job. There may be a personal problem such as a serious family illness or even involvement in a serious accident which has occurred preventing them from getting in touch.

It is safer not to assume that the employee has simply "resigned" but to try to establish what the employee's intentions are if at all possible.

The first step is to write to the employee at his/her last known address referring to his/her absence and lack of contact and asking him/her to get in touch regarding his/her intentions. If there is no reply then a further letter should be sent, preferably recorded delivery, giving a reasonable deadline for reply and advising that unless there is a reasonable explanation for the conduct then the company will be left with no alternative but to assume that the employee has repudiated his/her contract and that the employment will be treated as terminated.

If the employee does get in touch, then it will be for the company to decide whether the employee's explanation of the circumstances is acceptable and whether disciplinary action/dismissal is appropriate.

Drinking, Drugs and Substance Abuse

Dealing with employees whose behaviour or standard of work is impaired as a result of drinking, taking drugs or substance abuse may be dealt with either on the grounds of capability or conduct, depending upon the circumstances.

In the more straightforward and possibly more frequent cases of individuals simply getting drunk or recklessly abusing drugs or substances to the extent that work is affected, the normal approach would be to deal with such issues in the normal way as for any other breach of conduct, i.e. by giving disciplinary warnings which may lead to dismissal. Ideally the company's disciplinary rules and procedures should spell out that these are examples of unacceptable conduct.

In situations where serious recklessness could result in possible danger or a serious breach of the health and safety

rules then summary dismissal may be appropriate. Under these circumstances warning of this should be included in the examples of "gross" misconduct so that employees are aware of the severity with which such actions would be regarded.

However, if there is a longer term problem of alcoholism, drug-taking or substance abuse then the matter should be dealt with as a sickness problem. The employee should be offered time off for medical help and counselling so that every effort can be made to help the employee to recover. If the employee will not accept the help that is being offered and refuses to co-operate or recognise the problem then the employer will be left with little choice but to proceed down the disciplinary path for not meeting standards of performance. If the employee can be persuaded to co-operate then the prospects of rehabilitation and recovery can be assessed before considering whether disciplinary action/dismissal need be considered.

Rescinding of Notice

Occasionally an employee may resign, either verbally or in writing, and then expect the employer to agree to rescind it. Whether or not the employer is required to do so depends on a variety of factors.

If an employee has tendered his/her resignation and simply changes his/her mind some time later then it is up to the employer whether or not he/she wishes to allow the notice to be withdrawn. It may be that a replacement has already been found or alternative arrangements made.

If an employee resigns in the heat of the moment, for example, following a row with his/her supervisor or perhaps when he/she were physically or mentally not well enough to appreciate his/her actions, the employer should check with the employee whether he/she really do wish to resign. If there is any doubt then a cooling off period should be allowed followed by a request to put the notice in writing.

In the case of Greater Glasgow Health Board v Mackay EAT Ms Mackay said she intended to leave and wrote out an apparently unequivocal letter of resignation. She then sent in sick notes and tried to withdraw her notice.

EAT upheld the Tribunal's view that she was suffering from stress and anxiety state and that she had not rationally and genuinely submitted her resignation. They felt that the employer would have known that she was suffering from stress when she gave in her notice and because the employer refused to allow the notice to be withdrawn she was regarded as having been unfairly dismissed.

Changing the Date of Termination

Once an employer has given an employee notice of termination of employment then it must stand.

If the employer wishes the employee to work beyond the termination date then it must be with the agreement of the employee.

If the employer wishes to bring forward the termination date then payment in lieu must be made for the weeks of notice which the employee is not required to work.

If an employee gives the employer his/her resignation but the employer wishes to bring the date forward, then the termination will be turned into a dismissal.

Maternity

Dismissal of an employee because she is pregnant or for any other reason connected with her pregnancy will automatically be regarded as an unfair dismissal.

There are two exceptions:

1 The employee is incapable of adequately doing the work she is employed to do
2 Because of her pregnancy the employee cannot continue to work without contravening a statute or other enactment

Even if these exceptions apply the organisation must satisfy the test of reasonableness including first trying to find suitable alternative work or where possible make suitable alternative arrangements.

An employee who is entitled to return to work following her maternity leave and complies with the rules and regulations relating to her right to return but is not allowed to do so by her employer, will be regarded as having been dismissed.

Basically, an employee is entitled to return to work in the job in which she was employed under her contract of employment and on terms and conditions of employment not less favourable than those which would have been applicable had she not been absent. This does not have to be exactly the same job but must be similar in terms of responsibility, status, salary and benefits, etc. This means that if the employer offers her less favourable terms and/or a different job than existed before the maternity leave then this will be regarded as a dismissal and will leave the way open for the employee to claim unfair dismissal.

There is an exception for organisations employing five or less employees, including any associated companies, whereby if they can demonstrate that it was not reasonably practicable to allow the person to return to work nor was it reasonably practicable to offer alternative work then the employer can exclude the employee's right to complain of unfair dismissal although there may still be an entitlement to a redundancy payment.

If as a result of a business re-organisation the employer is unable to offer the job which she was originally employed to do but instead offers suitable alternative work which the employee unreasonably refuses then there is deemed to be no dismissal.

Refusal to Obey a Reasonable Instruction

Although it is potentially fair for an employee to be dismissed for disobedience the Industrial Tribunal will normally consider

- whether the order given was lawful, i.e. if it fell within the employee's contractual obligations
- whether it was reasonable
- whether the employee was reasonable in refusing to obey

Whether an order was lawful will generally depend upon the circumstances and the terms under which the employee is employed, both written and implied terms. For example, normal hours of work, holiday entitlements, sickness benefits, shift patterns, should be recorded in the Written Statement of Terms and Conditions of Employment or may be contained in collective agreements or staff handbooks. Key duties may well be recorded in a job description although it would be impracticable to record every single possible duty that may need to be performed. Employees are also expected at common law to obey all legitimate and reasonable instructions and co-operate with the employer in the performance of their jobs.

For example, in Glitz v Watford Electric Co Ltd EAT 1979, Ms Glitz was employed as a copy typist/general clerical duties clerk. After some three years her employers asked her to take on the operating of the duplicating machine. She refused and her dismissal was deemed to be fair because her new duty was considered to fall within the range of general clerical duties and therefore it was reasonable of the employer to expect her to comply.

If an employee refuses to carry out a reasonable instruction, then the employee should be consulted and the reason for the disobedience considered so that his/her views can be taken into account. If the employee continues to refuse then the disciplinary warnings procedure should be adopted, advising the employee that dismissal could result if he/she continues to refuse.

Typical examples of disobedience include:

- Refusing to attend training courses where the training is essential to improve the employee's standard of performance or where it is necessary to meet operational needs
- Refusing to work overtime even where there is no specific term in the contract may be considered to be unreasonable if the business needs are such that the refusal would create operating difficulties
- Refusing to accept changed duties or hours of work to meet necessary changes in the operational requirements of the business
- Refusing to comply with the standards of dress required, e.g. wearing a shirt and tie

Smoking

An employee has no implied right to smoke in the workplace.

Increasingly, more and more employers are introducing no smoking policies in the workplace. In Dryden v Greater Glasgow Health Board it was found that Ms Dryden had not been constructively dismissed because of her resignation as a result of her employer introducing a smoking ban. The employer had consulted widely, had given reasonable notice of the change and had offered counselling and support to employees wishing help to give up smoking.

Trade Union Membership/Non-membership and Activities

Dismissal because of an employee's trade union membership or non-trade union membership or proposal to join or not to join a trade union is automatically unfair.

An employee who is dismissed for taking part in industrial action, even if the recognised trade union has carried out the correct balloting procedures beforehand, is not protected from unfair dismissal unless he/she can demonstrate that other employees were dismissed under similar circumstances and have subsequently been reinstated by the employer.

Redundancy

Definition of redundancy

Redundancy is defined as dismissal because:

- The employer has ceased or intends to cease to carry on the business for the purpose for which the employee has been employed or to carry on the business in the place where the employee was employed or
- The requirements of the business for the employee to carry out work of a particular kind or to carry out work of a particular kind in the place where the employee was employed has ceased or diminished or is expected to cease or diminish

Employees who are under their company's normal retirement age and have two years' continuous service working 16 hours or more per week (or have five years' continuous service working 8 hours but less than 16 hours per week) from the age of 18 are entitled to a statutory redundancy payment on termination of employment as a result of redundancy.

The amount of the statutory redundancy payment is based on actual weekly pay up to a maximum amount which is set by the State and is calculated on the basis of the individual's age and complete years of service to a maximum of 20 years.

For the year 1992/93 the maximum statutory redundancy payment has been set at £205 per week. This amount is reviewed in April of each year.

To ensure that redundancy is deemed to be a fair reason for dismissal the following steps should be taken:

1 **Consultation**

Consultation should begin at the earliest opportunity as soon as it has been established that there will have to be dismissals for reasons of redundancy.

With some minor exceptions, e.g. agency temporaries, partners in the firm, all staff should be included in the consultation process. This includes part-timers, employees with short service, home-workers, employees on maternity leave, employees over retirement age, employees who normally work in the UK but are currently working abroad and even YTS employees if they are under a contract of employment.

If a trade union is recognised by the employer then there are minimum periods of consultation that must be complied with dependent upon the numbers of employees to be made redundant, i.e.

Less than 10 employees   as soon as possible

10 or more employees to be made
redundant within 30 days or less   } 30 days

$$\left.\begin{array}{l}\text{100 or more employees to be made}\\\text{redundant within 90 days or less}\end{array}\right\}\ \text{90 days}$$

The following information should be disclosed in writing to the trade union:

- the reasons for the proposals
- numbers and descriptions of the employees affected
- total number of employees of each description
- proposed method of selection
- proposed method of carrying out the dismissals and when

Good reasons must be given to the trade union for rejecting any representations that are put forward.

2 Personal consultation

Whether or not there is a recognised trade union the employees affected by redundancy are entitled to be consulted personally.

3 Fair selection for redundancy

Dismissal for reasons of redundancy may be seen to be unfair if the reason for the redundancy could be applied equally to other employees in the organisation who were not dismissed.

If there is an agreed procedure or if custom and practice has been established in selecting those to be made redundant then this should be followed to ensure fairness and consistency.

If there is no established practice for selection then the selection criteria should be agreed in advance with the trade union or staff representatives where they exist.

Even if there is no staff representation the selection criteria should be determined prior to the selection process to ensure fairness and consistency.

The following criteria are now commonly used to select employees for redundancy, taking into account the changing business needs of the organisation:

- Skills and experience
- Ability and performance
- Absenteeism and attendance records
- Disciplinary records
- Length of service

When using any of the above criteria it is important for the organisation to be able to back up their decisions based on hard fact. For example, if poor attendance was used as a selection criteria and yet the individual selected because of his/her poor attendance had never been formally spoken to about it, this would not be seen by an Industrial Tribunal as a genuine reason for selection as the poor attendance had not been treated as an important issue in the past such as to warrant corrective action. Therefore to use it as a selection criteria would be seen to be unfair.

4 Alternative Work

Every attempt should be made to offer suitable alternative work to those whose jobs are to be made redundant. It is advisable for the employer to ask the individual for his/her own views as to what might be considered suitable so that all options can be explored even when there appears to be no other work available. The possibility of offering training to be able to undertake alternative work within the organisation should also be considered.

Alternative work should be sought throughout the organisation and associated companies, not just the particular establishment concerned. For example, if there are two or three branches of, say, a Travel Agent or Hardware Shop then the employer should check all branches when seeking alternative work for a redundant employee.

Employees accepting alternative work in the face of redundancy are entitled to a statutory trial period of four weeks. If they decide during the trial period that the new job is unsuitable then they retain their right to a statutory redundancy payment. If the employee unreasonably refuses an offer of suitable alternative work then the dismissal stands and they will lose their entitlement to a statutory redundancy payment.

5 Right to appeal

A facility should be made known and available to employees affected by redundancy so that if they feel they have been unfairly selected they can formally make a complaint.

Where there is a staff association or a trade union is recognised, the appeals panel should include staff and/or trade union representatives as well as employer representatives. Where there is no staff representation then ideally the panel should consist of employer representatives who ideally were not directly involved with the initial selection of the employee raising the complaint.

Contravention of some Statutory Requirement

Dismissal for contravening a statutory requirement is a fair reason for dismissal provided that it is handled fairly and consistently.

One of the most common examples of an employee becoming unable to meet a statutory requirement to perform his/her job is the loss of a driving licence by an individual who is employed as a driver.

Before taking the decision to dismiss, the organisation should consider and discuss with the employee concerned:

- The reasons for the loss
- How long the driving ban is for
- Whether there is any chance of an appeal succeeding
- What alternative work could be offered during the period of the driving ban

- What alternative arrangements could be made to enable the employee to continue his/her work
- The employee's previous track record
- Any mitigitating circumstances raised by the employee

The above considerations will clearly have different repercussions for different organisations depending upon the nature of the employer's business, size of organisation and numbers of employees.

As with all dismissals, the employee should have the right of appeal, ideally to a more senior person in the organisation who was not party to the decision to dismiss.

Some other substantial reason

Dismissal for "some other substantial reason" may cover any dismissals which do not fall under the previous four headings (i.e. conduct, capability, redundancy and contravention of a statutory requirement) and which are nevertheless substantial and justifiable but not trivial or frivolous.

Some frequent examples of dismissal for SOSR are:

1 Business re-organisations

Providing an organisation is able to demonstrate that it has sound, good business reasons for re-organising the way their work is carried out then a dismissal resulting from an employee refusing to accept the changes may be seen to be a fair dismissal.

Before dismissal is considered the employer should consult fully with the staff representatives and/or trade union representatives and the employees themselves.

Any representations should be fully considered and responded to and every attempt to reach agreement made.

For example changes in duties or re-organisation of the work teams.

2 Changes to terms and conditions of employment

As above, providing the organisation can show that it has good, sound business reasons for introducing the changes and that every attempt has been made to reach agreement through consultations and discussions then dismissal will be seen to be fair.

For example, changes to the pattern of working hours, changes in the construction of the earnings package, the requirement to work compulsory overtime.

3 Conflicts of interest

If an organisation believes that there is a genuine commercial risk as a result of close relationships between their own employees and that of their competitors or even within their own organisation then dismissal may be seen to be fair although it is important to see whether suitable alternative work may be offered as an alternative to dismissal.

For example, if an employee has access to confidential information which in the wrong hands could be damaging to his/her employer and his/her spouse works for a rival company where the information could be of value, then the employer's fears could justify the dismissal.

4 Working relationships

Occasionally working relationships deteriorate to such

an extent that the performance of the business is detrimentally affected.

For example, a serious personality clash where the individual concerned can be properly identified as the cause of the problem.

5 Criminal offences

If the commitment of a criminal offence outside the working environment affects the integrity and standing of the business then dismissal for some other substantial reason rather than for gross misconduct may be seen to be fair.

For example, an employee convicted of child molesting would not be a suitable individual to continue to employ in positions where he/she was required to visit clients in their homes or as a park attendant. If he/she was employed in an office job where there was no potential contact with members of the public then there would be no justification on that count to dismiss. The reactions of the workforce however may be such that the working relationship has irretrievably broken down because of the nature of the offence in which case dismissal may be inevitable.

Often, where a criminal conviction occurs for off duty conduct, the conviction itself may be the first knowledge that the employer has of the offence. However, it is not necessary to wait for conviction before considering whether dismissal is appropriate and EAT has said that it is usual for employers to rely on hearsay evidence such as police reports when carrying out their investigations.

Whether or not the employee is found guilty of the

criminal offence is not sufficient in itself for the incident to automatically warrant dismissal. The key issue is whether the conviction will have an adverse affect on the employment relationship or whether it may be detrimental to the reputation or performance of the business.

6 Dismissal of one party to a partnership arrangement

It is not unusual for husbands and wives to be employed in a partnership arrangement, e.g. Stewards of a Golf Club or private club, or as wardens in a residential home where "living in" is part of the terms and conditions of employment.

If one of the parties decides to leave or his/her employment is terminated then it may be fair for the remaining partner to be dismissed if he/she has been employed on joint contracts.

In Provins & Provins v Martin the Newsagent Ltd, Mr & Mrs Provins were employed as a team with accommodation provided. Mr Provins was fairly dismissed for capability and Mrs Provins was subsequently fairly dismissed for SOSR because it was established that the two employments stood or fell together.

Even if they have been employed as a team the issue may not be so simple. For example, in Great Mountain and Tumble Rugby Football Club v Howlett EAT there was a row between Mr & Mrs Howlett following which Mrs Howlett resigned. The employers notified Mr Howlett that when his wife's notice expired he would be in breach of contract and dismissed him. EAT upheld the view that, even though there was a written agreement to the effect that the appointments were a joint appointment of a husband and wife team, if either gave notice it would terminate the agreement. Mrs Howlett's duties were so minimal that it was felt that her absence would not have made a substantial difference and the dismissal was therefore unfair.

7 Non-disclosure of a medical condition

If an employee deliberately withholds information concerning a medical condition which could adversely affect his/her future capability to do the job, then dismissal may be seen to be fair.

For example, an individual who has successfully applied for a warehouse job which involves lifting and carrying heavy loads and has purposely withheld the knowledge that he/she suffers from a slipped disc may be seen as a justifiable dismissal.

8 Pressure from a client company

More and more frequently organisations are putting their services such as catering, cleaning and security out to contractors.

Occasionally situations occur where the client company insists that one of the contractor's employees is removed and the contractor is unable to move the employee to a new site.

If the contractor has no alternative but to dismiss because the business is at risk if the request is refused, then the dismissal may be seen to be fair.

In all the above situations the employer will have been expected to have acted fairly and reasonably when reaching the decision to dismiss.

Consultation

The employee should be fully consulted about the circumstances and all options fully explored. His/her personal representations should be considered and attempts to reach agreement made before any decision is taken to dismiss.

For example it may be possible to move the employee to alternative work where his/her limitations are not an issue.

Time to adjust

Where appropriate, time to make alternative arrangements should be provided. For example, if an employee is to be dismissed because of a close relationships being established then it would be fair to allow time to enable that employee to find new work providing the delay does not give rise to further complications.

A typical example may be where a secretary marries her boss or another senior member of the organisation and it could be considered that "pillow talk" may be prejudicial to the efficient running of the business.

Written reasons for Dismissal

An employee with more than two years of continuous service, regardless of the number of hours that he/she work each week, is entitled to ask for and be given a written statement giving the reasons for his/her dismissal within 14 days of their request.

If the employer unreasonably refuses or provides a statement giving false or inadequate reasons for the dismissal the employee may complain to an Industrial Tribunal.

The complaint must be made within three months of the effective termination date. If the claim is upheld the Industrial Tribunal may make a declaration as to what it believes the reasons for the dismissal were and will award the employee compensation equivalent to two weeks' pay.

Constructive Dismissal

Constructive dismissal occurs when an employee resigns because the employer's actions towards him/her are such that to continue working has become untenable.

The following are typical examples of constructive dismissal:

- Telling an employee that if they don't resign they will be sacked
- Imposing a pay cut
- Imposing a loss of status
- Requiring the employee to consistently carry out unreasonable instructions or duties
- Treating the employee in a consistently unreasonable manner

Even though the employee has resigned he/she is still entitled to submit a claim to an Industrial Tribunal on the basis that they have been unfairly dismissed.

Complaints

Employees who wish to make a claim of unfair dismissal to an Industrial Tribunal must do so within three months of the date of their termination of employment.

The Industrial Tribunal will only hear complaints of Unfair

or Constructive Dismissal from individuals who are under the normal retirement age for their company and who have 2 years' continuous service working 16 hours or more per week (or have five years' continuous service working 8 but less than 16 hours per week).

Compensation

If an Industrial Tribunal finds that an employee has been unfairly dismissed they can order, if the employee wishes,

- Reinstatement to the same job or
- Re-engagement to a different job or
- Compensation

The basis of calculating the amount of compensation that can be awarded is set by the state and is reviewed in April of each year. The amounts shown are those set for the year April 1992/93.

Compensation is awarded on the following basis:

Type of Award	Possible Award
Basic award	£6,150 maximum

Calculated as for statutory redundancy but with no minimum age on the basis of actual earnings up to a maximum weekly amount set by the State. For the year 1992/93 this is set at £205.

Compensatory award	£10,000 maximum

Calculated to cover future losses both known and estimated, e.g. potential loss of earnings and benefits.

Additional award	£5,330 maximum

Calculated to compensate for an organisation's refusal to comply with an order to reinstate or re-engage the dismissed employee. For the year 1992/93 this is set at £205 per week.

Calculating Compensation

Basic Award

The basic award is intended to compensate an employee for the loss of job security and is calculated in exactly the same way as for a statutory redundancy payment taking into account age, length of service and the relevant amount for a week's pay up to the maximum amount set by statute, i.e.

- half a week's pay for each complete year in which the employee was less than 22 years old
- one week's pay for each complete year in which the employee was less than 41 but not less than 22 years old
- one and a half week's pay for each complete year in which the employee was 41 years old or more until age 65 or the company's normal retirement age whichever is sooner.

Service in excess of 20 years is excluded and the award is reduced by one-twelfth for each complete month of service after the employee's 64th birthday so that by age 65 there is no entitlement. This is known as tapering.

Calculating Continuous Service for the Basic Award

Continuous service is calculated by counting the complete years of service from the effective date of termination. The effective date of termination is:

■ where dismissal is with notice, the date on which the notice expires

■ if no notice or inadequate notice is given then the effective date of termination is the date on which statutory notice would have expired.

Reductions in the Basic Award

The basic award may reduced in the following circumstances:

1 If an employee has received a redundancy payment then the amount received may be deducted from the basic award.

2 If an employee has unreasonably refused an offer of reinstatement which included reinstating earnings and other benefits.

3 If the tribunal considers that the employee's conduct prior to the dismissal was such that it would be just and equitable to reduce the award.

The are two exceptions to this, i.e.:

- if selection for redundancy was for trade union reasons, which would automatically be considered as unfair, then there is a minimum basic award and only the amount by which this exceeds the normal basic award may be reduced or

- where dismissal was for trade union reasons the tribunal must disregard conduct leading to dismissal that was a breach of contractual term relating to trade union membership.

Calculation of a week's pay

A week's pay is defined as the contractual remuneration for working the normal working hours in the week. Overtime hours and overtime pay are excluded unless they are normally obligatory and guaranteed.

The following payments should be included:

- wages or salary
- contractual bonuses, allowances, shift premiums
- commission if this is a regular part of the earnings, e.g. as for sales representatives

The following should not be included:

- overtime unless it is a contractual requirement
- expenses, e.g. travel reimbursements, lodging allowances

- payments in kind, e.g. company car
- tips and gratuities except where there is a fixed service charge which is regarded as actual pay.

The formula for calculating a week's pay is normal working hours multiplied by the average hourly rate of remuneration. The average hourly rate is calculated by taking the average over the last 12 weeks.

For shift workers where earnings vary with the shift pattern and premium payable, the formula to calculate a week's pay is to take the average number of hours worked in a week multiplied by the average hourly rate of pay over the last 12 weeks.

If there are no normal working hours then the week's pay is calculated by taking the employee's average weekly earnings over the past 12 weeks.

Where earnings vary with work done then the week's pay is calculated by taking the normal working hours per week multiplied by the average hourly rate of remuneration averaged over the last 12 weeks.

Compensatory Award

The compensatory award is intended to reflect actual financial loss suffered by the employee and will take into account the following:

- loss of net earnings from the date of dismissal to the date of the tribunal hearing although earnings from any new employment will be taken into account
- estimated loss of earnings following the date of the hearing

- loss of employment protection rights, i.e. the need to accrue two years' continuous service with a new employer
- loss of pension rights
- loss of benefits such as company car, BUPA, cheap meals
- reasonable expenses incurred in looking for a new job

Tribunals have a fair amount of discretion allowing them to reduce the amount of compensatory award to reflect the percentage of contributory conduct of the employee.

For example, if the dismissal would have been seen as fair but for the procedure not being correctly followed then they may reduce the amount of compensation awarded to reflect this.

Normally if there is a reduction in the compensatory award to reflect the employee's conduct then in most cases the same reduction would be made to the basic award.

Mitigation of Loss

The compensatory award may be reduced if a dismissed employee does not take reasonable steps to mitigate his/her loss by making a reasonable effort to find suitable new employment. Clearly, an individual's personal circumstances will have an effect on how easy it will be for him/her to find new work, for example, his/her age or state of health may be a factor. The state of the job market will also be taken into account when considering what the individual should be able to achieve in terms of new employment.

The burden of proof will be on the employer to show that the dismissed employee has failed to mitigate his/her loss. If the tribunal agrees with the employer then a view will be taken as to when the individual could reasonably have been expected to have found a suitable job and the estimated earnings will be taken into account when calculating compensation.

Ex Gratia and Redundancy Payments

Ex gratia payments made by an employer must be offset against the compensatory award. If the reason for dismissal is for redundancy then any redundancy payment made in excess of the statutory redundancy payment will be offset against the compensatory award.

Ex gratia payments will not necessarily be offset against the basic award unless the employer has clearly stated when making the payment that it was intended to meet any future liability arising out of the termination of the employment.

If a payment was made without any clarification then it may be taken by the tribunal as being made as a general payment or an *ex gratia* payment which may be construed as being intended to reflect past years of service and not as compensation for future loss.

Additional Awards

An additional award may be made to compensate when the tribunal has ordered reinstatement or re-engagement but the employer has failed to comply even though there was no practicable reason why he/she should not do so.

There are two levels of additional award

- between 13 – 26 weeks' pay
  for cases of ordinary unfair dismissal
- between 26 – 52 weeks' pay
  for cases where dismissal amounted to unlawful sex or race discrimination

Calculation of the Additional Award

A week's pay for the calculation of the additional award is calculated in the same way as for the basic award.

The tribunals have a fair amount of discretion in determining the amount of the award taking into account the circumstances of the case.

Special Awards

Calculated to compensate for unfair dismissal on grounds of union membership or activities, unfairly dismissed for non-membership of a trade union or unfairly selected for redundancy on the grounds of trade union membership or activity. Minimum basic award of £2700 for the year 1992/93.

£6150 maximum

Where reinstatement or re-engagement is requested but not ordered. One week's pay x 104 or £13,400, as at 1992/93, whichever is greater.

£26,800 maximum

If reinstatement or re-engagement is ordered but the employer refuses to comply. One week's pay x 156 or £20,100, as at 1992/93, whichever is greater.

No limit

The special award may be reduced if the tribunal considers that the employee contributed to the dismissal by his/her conduct, or if the employee refused an offer to be reinstated or prevented an order for reinstatement or re-engagement from being complied with.

Appendix 1

Example Disciplinary Procedure

1 Purpose of the Procedure

The purpose of the Disciplinary Rules and Procedures is to help and encourage all employees to achieve and maintain the desired standards of conduct and performance and to ensure consistency and fairness in the treatment of all employees in meeting these objectives.

2 Principles

At each stage of the procedure the employee will be notified of the nature of the complaint against him/her in advance of the disciplinary hearing.

Employees whose conduct or performance is below the standards required by the organisation will be given the opportunity to improve before getting into serious difficulty by being offered advice and guidance or further training as may be appropriate.

No disciplinary action will be taken until the employee has been given the opportunity of putting forward his/her side of the case and the matter has been fully investigated.

The procedure may be instigated at any stage depending upon the seriousness of the employee's misconduct.

No employee will be dismissed for a first breach of discipline except in the case of gross misconduct when the outcome will be summary dismissal without notice or payment in lieu of notice.

All employees will have the right to appeal against any disciplinary action taken against them.

3 Procedure

Informal Discussions

Before taking formal disciplinary action every effort should be made to resolve the matter by informal discussion between the employee concerned and his/her immediate line management. Only where this fails to bring about the desired improvement should the formal disciplinary procedure be implemented.

Stage One – Oral Warning

If, despite informal discussions, conduct or performance does not meet acceptable standards then the employee will be given a formal Oral Warning by his/her immediate Supervisor.

The employee will be advised of the reason for the

warning and that it is the first stage of the disciplinary procedure. The warning will remain on file for six months following which it will be disregarded provided that satisfactory conduct or performance has been achieved and maintained.

The employee may, if he/she wishes, be accompanied by his/her staff representative, shop steward or a work colleague of his/her choice.

Notes of the interview will be taken and a copy passed to the employee concerned.

If the employee wishes to appeal against the disciplinary action taken then he/she should do so within five working days of the warning being given, in writing, to his/her immediate Department Manager.

Stage Two – First Written Warning

If the matters previously complained of have not been resolved or in the case of more serious breaches of standards, whether previously complained of or not, a First Written Warning will be given by the Department Manager.

The employee will be advised of the reason for the warning and that it is a First Written Warning under the Disciplinary Procedure. The warning will remain on file for twelve months following which it will be disregarded if the necessary improvements in conduct or performance have been achieved and maintained.

The employee may, if he/she wishes, be accompanied by his/her staff representative, shop steward or a work colleague of his/her choice.

A letter summarising the discussions will be given to the employee concerned.

If the employee wishes to appeal against the disciplinary action taken then he/she should do so within five working days of the warning's being given, in writing, to his/her appropriate Senior Manager.

Stage Three – Final Written Warning

If the matters previously complained of have not been resolved or in the case of very serious breaches of standards, whether previously complained of or not, a Final Written Warning will be given by his/her appropriate Senior Manager.

The employee will be advised of the reason for the warning and that it is a Final Written Warning under the Disciplinary Procedure. The warning will remain on file for two years following which it will be disregarded if the necessary improvements in conduct and performance have been achieved and maintained.

The employee may, if he/she wishes, be accompanied by a staff representative, shop steward or a work colleague of his/her choice.

A letter summarising the discussions will be given to the employee concerned.

If the employee wishes to appeal against the disciplinary action taken then he/she should do so within five working days of the warning being given, in writing, to his/her appropriate Head of Department.

Stage Four – Dismissal

If the matters previously complained of have not been resolved or in the event of very serious misconduct then the employee will be dismissed by his/her appropriate Head of Department.

The employee will be advised of the reason for the dismissal and the period of notice to which he/she is entitled under the terms of their contract.

If requested by the employee, written reasons for the dismissal will be given within two weeks of the request.

The employee may, if he/she wishes, be accompanied at the hearing by a staff representative, shop steward or a work colleague of his/her choice.

If the employee wishes to appeal against the decision to dismiss then he/she should do so within five working days of the date of termination of employment, in writing, to the Chief Executive.

Examples of Conduct which may lead to dismissal following disciplinary action:

- Poor attendance/timekeeping
- Unreasonable absenteeism
- Poor work performance
- Carelessness/negligence
- Refusal to obey reasonable instructions
- Behaviour which is likely to disrupt working relationships or relationships with clients
- Failure to observe Health and Safety requirements

4 Gross Misconduct

If an employee is accused of an act of gross misconduct then the following procedure will apply:

Suspension

■ If necessary, the employee may be suspended on full pay, normally for not more than five working days, to enable a full investigation to be carried out

Dismissal

■ If following investigation the company is satisfied that gross misconduct has occurred then the employee will be dismissed summarily, without notice and without payment in lieu of notice

The employee will be advised of the reasons for the dismissal and that he/she is not entitled to be given notice of termination of employment or payment in lieu of notice.

If requested by the employee, written reasons for the dismissal will be provided within two weeks of the request.

If he/she wishes, he/she may be accompanied by a staff representative, shop steward or a work colleague of his/her choice.

If the employee wishes to appeal against the decision to dismiss then he/she must do so, in writing, within five working days of the date of termination of employment to the Managing Director whose decision will be final.

Examples of Gross Misconduct which may lead to Summary Dismissal:

- Theft
- Fraud
- Assault on a colleague or client
- Gross negligence
- Serious disregard of Health and Safety requirements
- Sex or Race Discrimination
- Conduct prejudicial to the company's reputation

5 Appeals

Following an appeal against disciplinary action the disciplinary action imposed will be reviewed wherever possible within five working days of the appeal's being received and it may either be:

- Confirmed or
- Rescinded but not increased

The employee will be notified of the outcome of his/her appeal, in writing, within five working days of the appeal having been heard.

6 Reinstatement

If an employee is reinstated following an appeal against dismissal, then the employee will be paid his/her normal earnings from the date of termination of employment until the date of reinstatement. All employment rights and company benefits will continue to accrue on the basis that service has not been broken as a result of the dismissal and reinstatement.

2

Appendix 2

Example Grievance Procedure

1 Purpose of the Procedure

The purpose of the Grievance Procedure is to enable all employees who feel that they have a complaint against any matter concerning their employment to be able to raise that matter with successive levels of management in an endeavour to resolve the issue to their satisfaction.

2 Principles

At each stage of the procedure the employee will be required to put his/her complaint in writing stating that he/she wishes to follow the Grievance Procedure and setting out brief details concerning his/her complaint.

At each stage of the procedure every effort will be made by both parties to reach agreement amicably and as speedily as possible.

Where a complaint has been raised and has not been resolved, the procedure provides scope for the complaint to be raised with the next level of management so that a fresh hearing takes place.

3 Procedure

Informal Discussions

Before pursuing a complaint through the Grievance Procedure the employee should raise any matters of dissatisfaction with his/her immediate supervisor. Only where this fails to bring about a satisfactory solution should the formal Grievance Procedure be pursued.

Stage One

If, despite informal discussions, the matter complained of has not been resolved then the employee should write to his/her immediate supervisor giving brief details concerning the nature of his/her complaint and stating that he/she wishes the matter to be pursued through the Grievance Procedure.

A meeting will be arranged with the supervisor, wherever practicable, within the next five working days in an endeavour to resolve the matter.

The employee may be represented at this meeting by his/her staff representative, shop steward, or a work colleague of his/her choice.

Notes should be kept of the meeting and a copy passed to the employee.

Stage Two

If the matter has not been resolved to the employee's satisfaction within, wherever possible, the next five working days then the matter may be raised in writing with the employee's Department Manager.

A meeting will be arranged with the Department Manager, wherever practicable, within the next five working days in an endeavour to resolve the matter.

The employee may be represented at this meeting by his/her staff representative, shop steward or a work colleague of his/her choice.

Notes should be kept of this meeting and a copy passed to the employee.

Stage Three

If the matter has not been resolved to the employee's satisfaction within, wherever possible, the next five working days then the matter may be raised in writing with the employee's appropriate Senior Manager.

A meeting will be arranged with the Senior Manager, wherever practicable, within the next five working days in an endeavour to resolve the matter.

The employee may be represented at this meeting by his/her staff representative, shop steward or a work colleague of his/her choice.

Notes should be kept of this meeting and a copy passed to the employee.

Stage Four

If the matter has still not been resolved to the employee's satisfaction within, wherever possible, the next five working days then the matter may be raised in writing with the Chief Executive whose decision will be final.

A meeting will be arranged with the Chief Executive, wherever practicable, within the next five working days in an endeavour to resolve the matter.

The employee may be represented at this meeting by his/her staff representative, shop steward or a work colleague of his/her choice.

Notes should be kept of this meeting and a copy passed to the employee.

3

Appendix 3

Example Complaints Procedure for Harassment

1 Purpose of the Procedure

The purpose of the Complaints Procedure for Harassment is to enable all employees who feel that they have a complaint of harassment against any person connected with their employment to be able to raise that complaint, in confidence, in an endeavour to resolve the issue to their satisfaction.

2 Principles

It is for each employee to determine what behaviour he/she finds offensive and what he/she finds acceptable. If the behaviour is unwanted then it will be regarded as harassment by the recipient whereas if the recipient finds the behaviour welcome then the behaviour will be considered friendly and wanted.

Harassment may occur as a result of one person's or a group of people's behaviour towards another which gives cause for offence. Such behaviour may be by a person of one sex to a person of the same sex or opposite sex or of one racial group to a person of the same or another racial group.

The employee may be required to put his/her complaint in writing and be prepared to supply evidence to a disciplinary hearing in an endeavour to resolve the matter equitably.

3 Procedure

Informal Discussions

Before pursuing the complaint through the Complaints Procedure for Harassment the employee should raise the matter with the harasser personally, making it clear that the behaviour is unwanted.

If the individual finds that it is too embarrassing or too difficult to do this personally then he/she may ask that a staff representative, shop steward where a trade union is recognised or work colleague of their choice speaks to the harasser on his/her behalf.

A note of the discussion should be recorded and kept by both the employee, his/her representative and the harasser.

Formal Complaint

If an informal approach to the harasser does not resolve the matter or if the matter complained of is of a more serious nature then the employee should speak directly to his/her immediate supervisor or where this is not possible to the next level of management.

The individual will be requested to provide details, in writing, of the complaint and of previous requests to the harasser to stop.

If the individual finds that the matter complained of is too embarrassing or it is too difficult to do this then he/she may ask his/her representative to act on his/her behalf or he/she may approach another member of management. For example, a female member of staff may prefer to take her complaint to a female manager.

If the complaint results in a disciplinary hearing then the individual must be willing to supply evidence to the hearing. This may be in person or in writing. The harassed employee's representative may be present at this meeting but will not be permitted to participate in any discussions unless specifically asked to do so.

4 Action by Management

The supervisor or manager with whom the complaint has been raised is responsible for ensuring that an investigation is carried out sensitively and discreetly at the earliest opportunity. If appropriate the investigation may be carried out by a more suitable designated person, for example in the case of sexual harassment by a person of the same sex as the harassed employee.

The supervisor or manager is responsible for notifying the alleged harasser in writing that a complaint has been made and by whom so that the person complained about may put forward his/her side of the case before it is decided whether the matter should be dealt with at a disciplinary hearing.

5 Disciplinary Action

If it is decided that the issue warrants a disciplinary hearing then the normal disciplinary rules and procedures will apply. The action taken will depend upon the seriousness of the offence, for example a minor offence could result in an oral warning being given whereas a very serious offence could result in summary dismissal.

6 Appeals

The person being disciplined will have the right to appeal by following the normal Disciplinary Appeals Procedure.

7 Outcome

Whatever the outcome the individual who raised the complaint will be informed in writing of what action has been taken, if any.

8 Confidentiality

All matters discussed must be treated in the strictest confidence by all those involved including the individual making the complaint as well as the alleged harasser.

9 Future Harassment or Victimisation

Any further proven harassment or victimisation by the same harasser will be regarded as a very serious offence and will be subject to disciplinary action which may lead to dismissal.

4

Appendix 4

Example Letter for Medical Report Permission

Employee Rights under the Access to Medical Reports Act 1988

1 You can ask to see the medical report before your company receives it. This request can be made either:

    1.1 to the company when you grant permission to obtain it in which case the company will advise your doctor of your request and let you know when to apply for the report or

    1.2 direct to the doctor at a later date but before the report is supplied to the company.

2 If you ask to see the report:

    2.1 you must contact your doctor to arrange access within 21 days of the company's applying for the report otherwise the doctor can give the report to the company without your consent. Under 1.2 above you must contact the doctor within 21 days of notifying that you wish to see the report.

2.2 having seen the report you can ask the doctor, in writing, to amend anything which you think is incorrect or misleading. If the doctor does not agree, a statement of your views will be attached to the report at your request.

2.3 provided you have seen it the report will not be given to the company without your consent.

3   You will not be entitled to see any part of the report which:

3.1 your doctor believes could seriously harm your physical or mental health or that of others

3.2 indicates the doctor's intentions where you are concerned

3.3 reveals information about another person or identity of someone who has given the doctor information about you unless that person consents or is a health professional involved with your care.

4   The doctor will tell you why access to any part of your report is refused. Your rights of amendment apply only to the disclosed parts of the report.

5   You do not have to give the company permission to obtain a medical report, however, the inability to obtain up-to-date medical information may affect decisons concerning your employment.

6   You may ask your doctor to allow you to see any medical report relating to you which he/she has provided for employment purposes in the last six months.

MEDICAL REPORT CONSENT FORM

Dear Mr/Mrs/Ms (Employee's Name)

I wish to obtain a medical report from your Doctor for the following purposes:

Chief Executive's signature:

Date:

To be completed by the employee and returned to the Chief Executive

To: Chief Executive

I confirm that I have been notified of my rights under the Access to Medical Reports Act 1988 and agree to the company requesting a medical report from my doctor/ consultant whose name and address is as follows:

Name

Address

I wish/do not wish to see the report.

Employee's signature

Date

Appendix 5

Maximum Awards of Compensation for Unfair Dismissal

Type of Award	1992/3	1993/4	1994/5
Basic award Calculated as for statutory redundancy but with no minimum age on the basis of actual earnings up to a maximum weekly amount of £205	£6,150		
Compensatory award Calculated to cover future losses both known and estimated, e.g. potential earnings and benefits	£10,000		
Additional award	£5,330		

Calculated to compensate for an organisation's refusal to comply with an order to reinstate or re-engage the dismissed employee